RESUMES
FOR
LAW
CAREERS

Professional Resumes Series

RESUMES
FOR
LAW
CAREERS

The Editors of

VGM Career Horizons

Printed on recyclable paper

 **VGM Career Horizons**
a division of *NTC Publishing Group*
Lincolnwood, Illinois USA

ACKNOWLEDGMENT

We would like to acknowledge the assistance of Mark Satterfield in compiling and editing this book.

Library of Congress Cataloging-in Publication Data

Resumes for law careers/the editors of VGM Career Horizons.

   p. cm. — (VGM professional resumes series)
  ISBN 0-8442-4388-4
   1. Law—Vocational guidance—United States. 2. Résumés (Employment)
I. VGM Career Horizons (Firm) II. Series: VGM's professional resumes
series.
KF297.Z9R47 1995   95-778
808'.06634—dc20   CIP

Published by VGM Career Horizons, a division of NTC Publishing Group
4255 West Touhy Avenue
Lincolnwood (Chicago), Illinois 60646-1975, U.S.A.

5 6 7 8 9 0 VP 9 8 7 6 5 4 3 2 1

CONTENTS

Introduction

Your resume is your first impression on a prospective employer. Though you may be articulate, intelligent, and charming in person, a poor resume may prevent you from ever having the opportunity to demonstrate your interpersonal skills, because a poor resume may prevent you from every being called for an interview. While few people have ever been hired solely on the basis of their resume, a well-written, well-organized resume can go a long way toward helping you land an interview. Your resume's main purpose is to get you that interview. The rest is up to you and the employer. If you both feel that you are right for the job and the job is right for you, chances are you will be hired.

A resume must catch the reader's attention yet still be easy to read and to the point. Resume styles have changed over the years. Today, brief and focused resumes are preferred. No longer do employers have the patience, or the time, to review several pages of solid type. A resume should be only one page long, if possible, and never more than two pages. Time is a precious commodity in today's business world and the resume that is concise and straightforward will usually be the one that gets noticed

Let's not make the mistake, though, of assuming that writing a brief resume means that you can take less care in preparing it. A successful resume takes time and thought, and if you are willing to make the effort, the rewards are well worth it. Think of your resume as a sales tool with the product being you. You want to sell yourself to a prospective employer. This book is designed to help you prepare a resume that will help you further your career—to land that next job, or first job, or to return to the work force after years of absence. So, read on. Make the effort and reap the rewards that a strong resume can being to your career. Let's get to it!

Chapter One

THE ELEMENTS OF A GOOD RESUME

A winning resume is made of the elements that employers are most interested in seeing when reviewing a job applicant. These basic elements are the essential ingredients of a successful resume and become the actual sections of your resume. The following is a list of elements that may be used in a resume. Some are essential; some are optional. We will be discussing these in this chapter in order to give you a better understanding of each element's role in the makeup of your resume:

1. Heading
2. Objective
3. Work Experience
4. Education
5. Honors
6. Activities
7. Certificates and Licenses
8. Professional Memberships
9. Special Skills
10. Personal Information
11. References

The first step in preparing your resume is to gather together information about yourself and your past accomplishments. Later you will refine this information, rewrite it in the most effective language,and organize it into the most attractive layout. First, let's take a look at each of these important elements individually.

Heading

The heading may seem to be a simple enough element in your resume, but be careful not to take it lightly. The heading should be placed at the top of your resume and should include your name, home address, and telephone numbers. If you can take calls at your current place of business, include your business number, since most employers will attempt to contact you during the business day. If this is not possible, or if you can afford it, purchase an answering machine that allows you to retrieve your messages while you are away from home. This way you can make sure you don't miss important phone calls. Always include your phone number on your resume. It is crucial that when prospective employers need to have immediate contact with you, they can.

Objective

When seeking a particular career path, it is important to list a job objective on your resume. This statement helps employers know the direction that you see yourself heading, so that they can determine whether your goals are in line with the position available. The objective is normally one sentence long and describes your employment goals clearly and concisely. See the sample resumes in this book for examples of objective statements.

The job objective will vary depending on the type of person you are, the field you are in, and the type of goals you have. It can be either specific or general, but it should always be to the point.

In some cases, this element is not necessary, but usually it is a good idea to include your objective. It gives your possible future employer an idea of where you are coming from and where you want to go.

The objective statement is better left out, however, if you are uncertain of the exact title of the job you seek. In such a case, the inclusion of an overly specific objective statement could result in your not being considered for a variety of acceptable positions; you should be sure to incorporate this information in your cover letter, instead.

Work Experience

This element is arguably the most important of them all. It will provide the central focus of your resume, so it is necessary that this section be as complete as possible. Only by examining your work experience in depth can you get to the heart of your accomplishments and present them in a way that demonstrates the strength of your qualifications. Of course, someone just out of school will have less work experience than someone who has been working for a number of years, but the amount of information isn't the most important thing—rather, how it is presented and how it highlights you as a person and as a worker will be what counts.

As you work on this section of your resume, be aware of the need for accuracy. You'll want to include all necessary information about each of your jobs, including job title, dates, employer, city, state, responsibilities, special projects, and accomplishments. Be sure to only list company accomplishments for which you were directly responsible. If you haven't participated in any special projects, that's all right—this area may not be relevant to certain jobs.

The most common way to list your work experience is in *reverse chronological order*. In other words, start with your most recent job and work your way backwards. This way your prospective employer sees your current (and often most important) job before seeing your past jobs. Your most recent position, if the most important, should also be the one that includes the most information, as compared to your previous positions. If you are just out of school, show your summer employment and part-time work, though in this case your education will most likely be more important than your work experience.

The following worksheets will help you gather information about your past jobs.

WORK EXPERIENCE
Job One:

Job Title _____

Dates _____

Employer _____

City, State _____

Major Duties _____

_____

_____

_____

_____

_____

_____

_____

Special Projects _____

_____

_____

Accomplishments _____

_____

_____

_____

_____

_____

_____

_____

Job Two:

Job Title _____

Dates _____

Employer _____

City, State _____

Major Duties _____

_____

_____

_____

_____

_____

_____

_____

Special Projects _____

_____

_____

_____

Accomplishments_____

_____

_____

_____

_____

_____

_____

_____

Job Three:

Job Title _____

Dates _____

Employer _____

City, State _____

Major Duties _____

_____

_____

_____

_____

_____

_____

_____

Special Projects _____

_____

_____

_____

Accomplishments_____

_____

_____

_____

_____

_____

_____

_____

Job Four:

Job Title _____

Dates _____

Employer _____

City, State _____

Major Duties _____

_____

_____

_____

_____

_____

_____

_____

Special Projects _____

_____

_____

_____

Accomplishments_____

_____

_____

_____

_____

_____

_____

_____

_____

Education

Education is the second most important element of a resume. Your educational background is often a deciding factor in an employer's decision to hire you. Be sure to stress your accomplishments in school with the same finesse that you stressed your accomplishments at work. If you are looking for your first job, your education will be your greatest asset, since your work experience will most likely be minimal. In this case, the education section becomes the most important. You will want to be sure to include any degrees or certificates you received, your major area of concentration, any honors, and any relevant activities. Again, be sure to list your most recent schooling first. If you have completed graduate-level work, begin with that and work in reverse chronological order through your undergraduate education. If you have completed an undergraduate degree, you may choose whether to list your high school experience or not. This should be done only if your high school grade-point average was well above average.

The following worksheets will help you gather information for this section of your resume. Also included are supplemental worksheets for honors and for activities. Sometimes honors and activities are listed in a section separate from education, most often near the end of the resume.

EDUCATION

School _____

Major or Area of Concentration _____

Degree _____

Date _____

School _____

Major or Area of Concentration _____

Degree _____

Date _____

Honors

Here, you should list any awards, honors, or memberships in honorary societies that you have received. Usually these are of an academic nature, but they can also be for special achievement in sports, clubs, or other school activities. Always be sure to include the name of the organization honoring you and the date(s) received. Use the worksheet below to help gather your honors information.

HONORS

Honor: _____

Awarding Organization: _____

Date(s): _____

Honor: _____

Awarding Organization: _____

Date(s): _____

Honor: _____

Awarding Organization: _____

Date(s): _____

Honor: _____

Awarding Organization: _____

Date(s): _____

Activities

You may have been active in different organizations or clubs during your years at school; often an employer will look at such involvement as evidence of initiative and dedication. Your ability to take an active role, and even a leadership role, in a group should be included on your resume. Use the worksheet provided to list your activities and accomplishments in this area. In general, you should exclude any organization the name of which indicates the race, creed, sex, age, marital status, color, or nation of origin of its members.

ACTIVITIES

Organization/Activity: _____

Accomplishments: _____

_____

_____

Organization/Activity: _____

Accomplishments: _____

_____

_____

Organization/Activity: _____

Accomplishments: _____

_____

_____

Organization/Activity: _____

Accomplishments: _____

_____

_____

As your work experience increases through the years, your school activities and honors will play less of a role in your resume, and eventually you will most likely only list your degree and any major honors you received. This is due to the fact that, as time goes by, your job performance becomes the most important element in your resume. Through time, your resume should change to reflect this.

Certificates and Licenses

The next potential element of your resume is certificates and licenses. You should list these if the job you are seeking requires them and you, of course, have acquired them. If you have applied for a license, but have not yet received it, use the phrase "application pending."

License requirements vary by state. If you have moved or you are planning to move to another state, be sure to check with the appropriate board or licensing agency in the state in which you are applying for work to be sure that you are aware of all licensing requirements.

Always be sure that all of the information you list is completely accurate. Locate copies of your licenses and certificates and check the exact date and name of the accrediting agency. Use the following worksheet to list your licenses and certificates.

CERTIFICATES AND LICENSES

Name of License: _____

Licensing Agency: _____

Date Issued: _____

Name of License: _____

Licensing Agency: _____

Date Issued: _____

Name of License: _____

Licensing Agency: _____

Date Issued: _____

Professional Memberships

Another potential element in your resume is a section listing professional memberships. Use this section to list involvement in professional associations, unions, and similar organizations. It is to your advantage to list any professional memberships that pertain to the job you are seeking. Be sure to include the dates of your involvement and whether you took part in any special activities or held any offices within the organization. Use the following worksheet to gather your information.

PROFESSIONAL MEMBERSHIPS

Name of Organization: _____

Offices Held: _____

Activities: _____

Date(s): _____

Name of Organization: _____

Offices Held: _____

Activities: _____

Date(s): _____

Name of Organization: _____

Offices Held: _____

Activities: _____

Date(s): _____

Name of Organization: _____

Offices Held: _____

Activities: _____

Date(s): _____

Special Skills

This section of your resume is set aside for mentioning any special abilities you have that could relate to the job you are seeking. This is the part of your resume where you have the opportunity to demonstrate certain talents and experiences that are not necessarily a part of your educational or work experience. Common examples include fluency in a foreign language, or knowledge of a particular computer application.

Special skills can encompass a wide range of your talents—remember to be sure that whatever skills you list relate to the type of work you are looking for.

Personal Information

Some people include "Personal" information on their resumes. This is not generally recommended, but you might wish to include it if you think that something in your personal life, such as a hobby or talent, has some bearing on the position you are seeking. This type of information is often referred to at the beginning of an interview, when it is used as an "ice breaker." Of course, personal information regarding age, marital status, race, religion, or sexual preference should never appear on any resume.

References

References are not usually listed on the resume, but a prospective employer needs to know that you have references who may be contacted if necessary. All that is necessary to include in your resume regarding references is a sentence at the bottom stating, "References are available upon request." If a prospective employer requests a list of references, be sure to have one ready. Also, check with whomever you list to see if it is all right for you to use them as a reference. Forewarn them that they may receive a call regarding a reference for you. This way they can be prepared to give you the best reference possible.

Chapter Two

WRITING YOUR RESUME

*N*ow that you have gathered together all of the information for each of the sections of your resume, it's time to write out each section in a way that will get the attention of whoever is reviewing it. The type of language you use in your resume will affect its success. You want to take the information you have gathered and translate it into a language that will cause a potential employer to sit up and take notice.

Resume writing is not like expository writing or creative writing. It embodies a functional, direct writing style and focuses on the use of action words. By using action words in your writing, you more effectively stress past accomplishments. Action words help demonstrate your initiative and highlight your talents. Always use verbs that show strength and reflect the qualities of a "doer." By using action words, you characterize yourself as a person who takes action, and this will impress potential employers.

The following is a list of verbs commonly used in resume writing. Use this list to choose the action words that can help your re-sume become a strong one:

administered	introduced
advised	invented
analyzed	maintained
arranged	managed
assembled	met with
assumed responsibility	motivated
billed	negotiated
built	operated
carried out	orchestrated
channeled	ordered
collected	organized
communicated	oversaw
compiled	performed
completed	planned
conducted	prepared
contacted	presented
contracted	produced
coordinated	programmed
counseled	published
created	purchased
cut	recommended
designed	recorded
determined	reduced
developed	referred
directed	represented
dispatched	researched
distributed	reviewed
documented	saved
edited	screened
established	served as
expanded	served on
functioned as	sold
gathered	suggested
handled	supervised
hired	taught
implemented	tested
improved	trained
inspected	typed
interviewed	wrote

Now take a look at the information you put down on the work experience worksheets. Take that information and rewrite it in paragraph form, using verbs to highlight your actions and accomplishments. Let's look at an example, remembering that what matters here is the writing style, and not the particular job responsibilities given in our sample.

WORK EXPERIENCE
Regional Sales Manager

Manager of sales representatives from seven states. Responsible for twelve food chain accounts in the East. In charge of directing the sales force in planned selling toward specific goals. Supervisor and trainer of new sales representatives. Consulting for customers in the areas of inventory management and quality control.

Special Projects: Coordinator and sponsor of annual food industry sales seminar.

Accomplishments: Monthly regional volume went up 25 percent during my tenure while, at the same time, a proper sales/cost ratio was maintained. Customer/company relations improved significantly.

Below is the rewritten version of this information, using action words. Notice how much stronger it sounds.

WORK EXPERIENCE
Regional Sales Manager

Managed sales representatives from seven states. Handled twelve food chain accounts in the eastern United States. Directed the sales force in planned selling towards specific goals. Supervised and trained new sales representatives. Consulted for customers in the areas of inventory management and quality control. Coordinated and sponsored the annual Food Industry Seminar. Increased monthly regional volume 25 percent and helped to improve customer/company relations during my tenure.

Another way of constructing the work experience section is by using actual job descriptions. Job descriptions are rarely written using the proper resume language, but they do include all the information necessary to create this section of your resume. Take the description of one of the jobs your are including on your resume (if you have access to it), and turn it into an action-oriented paragraph. Below is an example of a job description followed by a version of the same description written using action words. Again, pay attention to the style of writing, as the details of your own work experience will be unique.

PUBLIC ADMINISTRATOR I

Responsibilities: Coordinate and direct public services to meet the needs of the nation, state, or community. Analyze problems; work with special committees and public agencies; recommend solutions to governing bodies.

Aptitudes and Skills: Ability to relate to and communicate with people; solve complex problems through analysis; plan, organize, and implement policies and programs. Knowledge of political systems; financial management; personnel administration; program evaluation; organizational theory.

WORK EXPERIENCE
Public Administrator I

Wrote pamphlets and conducted discussion groups to inform citizens of legislative processes and consumer issues. Organized and supervised 25 interviewers. Trained interviewers in effective communication skills.

Now that you have learned how to word your resume, you are ready for the next step in your quest for a winning resume: assembly and layout.

Chapter Three

ASSEMBLY AND LAYOUT

*A*t this point, you've gathered all the necessary information for your resume, and you've rewritten it using the language necessary to impress potential employers. Your next step is to assemble these elements in a logical order and then to lay them out on the page neatly and attractively in order to achieve the desired effect: getting that interview.

Assembly

The order of the elements in a resume makes a difference in its overall effect. Obviously, you would not want to put your name and address in the middle of the resume or your special skills section at the top. You want to put the elements in an order that stresses your most important achievements, not the less pertinent information. For example, if you recently graduated from school and have no full-time work experience, you will want to list your education before you list any part-time jobs you may have held during school. On the other hand, if you have been gainfully employed for several years and currently hold an important position in your company, you will want to list your work experience ahead of your education, which has become less pertinent with time.

There are some elements that are always included in your resume and some that are optional. Following is a list of essential and optional elements:

Essential	*Optional*
Name	Job Objective
Address	Honors
Phone Number	Special Skills
Work Experience	Professional Memberships
Education	Activities
References Phrase	Certificates and Licenses
	Personal Information

Your choice of optional sections depends on your own background and employment needs. Always use information that will put you and your abilities in a favorable light. If your honors are impressive, then be sure to include them in your resume. If your activities in school demonstrate particular talents necessary for the job you are seeking, then allow space for a section on activities. Each resume is unique, just as each person is unique.

Types of Resumes

So far, our discussion about resumes has involved the most common type—the *reverse chronological* resume, in which your most recent job is listed first and so on. This is the type of resume usually preferred by human resources directors, and it is the one most frequently used. However, in some cases this style of presentation is not the most effective way to highlight your skills and accomplishments.

For someone reentering the work force after many years or someone looking to change career fields, the *functional resume* may work best. This type of resume focuses more on achievement and less on the sequence of your work history. In the functional resume, your experience is presented by what you have accomplished and the skills you have developed in your past work.

A functional resume can be assembled from the same information you collected for your chronological resume. The main difference lies in how you organize this information. Essentially, the work experience section becomes two sections, with your job duties and accomplishments comprising one section and your employer's name, city, state, your position, and the dates employed making up another section. The first section is placed near the top of the resume, just below the job objective section, and can be called *Accomplishments* or *Achievements*. The second section, containing the bare essentials of your employment history, should come after the accomplishments section and can be titled *Work Experience* or *Employment History*. The other sections of your resume remain the same. The work experience section is the only one affected in the functional resume. By placing the section that focuses on your achievements first, you thereby draw attention to these achievements. This puts less emphasis on who you worked for and more emphasis on what you did and what you are capable of doing.

For someone changing careers, emphasis on skills and achievements is essential. The identities of previous employers, which may be unrelated to one's new job field, need to be downplayed. The functional resume accomplishes this task. For someone reentering the work force after many years, a functional resume is the obvious choice. If you lack full-time work experience, you will need to draw attention away from this fact and instead focus on your skills and abilities gained possibly through volunteer activities or part-time work. Education may also play a more important role in this resume.

Which type of resume is right for you will depend on your own personal circumstances. It may be helpful to create a chronological *and* a functional resume and then compare the two to find out which is more suitable. The sample resumes found in this book include both chronological and functional resumes. Use these resumes as guides to help you decide on the content and appearance of your own resume.

Layout

Once you have decided which elements to include in your resume and you have arranged them in an order that makes sense and emphasizes your achievements and abilities, then it is time to work on the physical layout of your resume.

There is no single appropriate layout that applies to every resume, but there are a few basic rules to follow in putting your resume on paper:

1. Leave a comfortable margin on the sides, top, and bottom of the page (usually 1 to 1½ inches).

2. Use appropriate spacing between the sections (usually 2 to 3 line spaces are adequate).

3. Be consistent in the *type* of headings you use for the different sections of your resume. For example, if you capitalize the heading EMPLOYMENT HISTORY, don't use initial capitals and underlining for a heading of equal importance, such as Education.

4. Always try to fit your resume onto one page. If you are having trouble fitting all your information onto one page, perhaps you are trying to say too much. Try to edit out any repetitive or unnecessary information or possibly shorten descriptions of earlier jobs. Be ruthless. Maybe you've included too many optional sections.

CHRONOLOGICAL RESUME

ALYSE GOMEZ
444 YARDLEY DRIVE
ARMONG, CT   67732   **(204)555-7629**

EXPERIENCE

1990 to
Present   **ASSISTANT COUNSEL, UNITED STATES SENATE**
                   COMMITTEE ON FOOD, BEVERAGE AND HUNGER

Recipient of the highly competitive Senator Fauste Fellowship for Ethics. Duties include proposing, drafting, and promoting legislation for the appropriate Subcommittees. Emphasis has been on competition, safety, and interstate issues and legislation.

1989   **SUMMER ASSOCIATE, OLD & LUBLICK**

Researched and drafted briefs and memoranda on antitrust, contract, and insurance issues. Projects included drafting a motion for a new trial and a motion for judgment notwithstanding the verdict on an $67.5 million judgment.

1988   **SUMMER ASSOCIATE, LATE, LUCK & LOUGHLIN**

Researched and wrote on constitutional issues, including obscenity and the ramifications of the First Amendment on land use law.

1987   **STUDENT INTERN, HOUSE OF REPRESENTATIVES**

Wrote speeches and press releases for legislators and compiled weekly legislative summaries for statewide distribution.

EDUCATION

UNIVERSITY OF HARTFORD, SCHOOL OF LAW
J.D. 1990
Class Rank 17/223
Order of the Coif
Managing Editor, Law School Review
Scholar at Law Scholarship
Recipient of highest grade in Antitrust

UNIVERSITY OF VERMONT
B.A. Political Science
Summa Cum Laude
Studied at Imperial College, University of London

FUNCTIONAL RESUME

MARK STALL
465 A POINTE WAY
LASTLEY, OR 01775   (617) 555-9988

LEGAL
EXPERIENCE: DARTON, GLARM & GORSTON, PORTLAND, OR
                       Summer Law Clerk: Conducted legal research and
prepared legal memoranda. Attended hearings and depositions involving
domestic relations issues.

                       OREGON DEPT. OF PERSONNEL
                       Office of the General Counsel. Drafted appellate
briefs, motions and other legal memoranda on behalf of the Secretary.
Evaluated evidentiary transcripts including legal and medical documents.

EDUCATION: OREGON UNIVERSITY SCHOOL OF LAW
                       Candidate for Juris Doctor Degree
                           Participant in Detroit College trial
                       advocacy program.
                           First year orientation counselor
                           Witness in pretrial litigation
                       program.
                           Top third of my class academically.

                       TEXAS STATE UNIVERSITY
                       B.A. Political Science & Psychology

OTHER
EMPLOYMENT: Retail sales clerk, health club program
                       coordinator, and student postal clerk.

ADDITIONAL: Fluent in Spanish, English, and German.
                       Proficient with both Macintosh and IBM
                       computers.

References are available upon request

Don't let the idea of having to tell every detail about your life get in the way of producing a resume that is simple and straightforward. The more compact your resume, the easier it will be to read and the better an impression it will make for you.

In some cases, the resume will not fit on a single page, even after extensive editing. In such cases, the resume should be printed on two pages so as not to compromise clarity or appearance. Each page of a two-page resume should be marked clearly with your name and the page number, e.g., "Judith Ramirez, page 1 of 2." The pages should then be stapled together.

Try experimenting with various layouts until you find one that looks good to you. Always show your final layout to other people and ask them what they like or dislike about it, and what impresses them most about your resume. Make sure that is what you want most to emphasize. If it isn't, you may want to consider making changes in your layout until the necessary information is emphasized. Use the sample resumes in this book to get some ideas for laying out your resume.

Putting Your Resume in Print

Your resume should be typed or printed on good quality 8½" × 11" bond paper. You want to make as good an impression as possible with your resume; therefore, quality paper is a necessity. If you have access to a word processor with a good printer, or know of someone who does, make use of it. Typewritten resumes should only be used when there are no other options available.

After you have produced a clean original, you will want to make duplicate copies of it. Usually a copy shop is your best bet for producing copies without smudges or streaks. Make sure you have the copy shop use quality bond paper for all copies of your resume. Ask for a sample copy before they run your entire order. After copies are made, check each copy for cleanliness and clarity.

Another more costly option is to have your resume typeset and printed by a printer. This will provide the most attractive resume of all. If you anticipate needing a lot of copies of your resume, the cost of having it typeset may be justified.

Proofreading

After you have finished typing the master copy of your resume and before you go to have it copied or printed, you must thoroughly check it for typing and spelling errors. Have several people read it over just in case you may have missed an error. Misspelled words and typing mistakes will not make a good impression on a prospective employer, as they are a bad reflection on your writing ability and your attention to detail. With thorough and conscientious proofreading, these mistakes can be avoided.

The following are some rules of capitalization and punctuation that may come in handy when proofreading your resume:

Rules of Capitalization

- Capitalize proper nouns, such as names of schools, colleges, and universities, names of companies, and brand names of products.

- Capitalize major words in the names and titles of books, tests, and articles that appear in the body of your resume.

- Capitalize words in major section headings of your resume.

- Do not capitalize words just because they seem important.

- When in doubt, consult a manual of style such as *Words Into Type* (Prentice-Hall), or *The Chicago Manual of Style* (The University of Chicago Press). Your local library can help you locate these and other reference books.

Rules of Punctuation

- Use a comma to separate words in a series.

- Use a semicolon to separate series of words that already include commas within the series.

- Use a semicolon to separate independent clauses that are not joined by a conjunction.

- Use a period to end a sentence.

- Use a colon to show that the examples or details that follow expand or amplify the preceding phrase.

- Avoid the use of dashes.

- Avoid the use of brackets.

- If you use any punctuation in an unusual way in your resume, be consistent in its use.

- Whenever you are uncertain, consult a style manual.

Chapter Four

THE COVER LETTER

*O*nce your resume has been assembled, laid out, and printed to your satisfaction, the next and final step before distribution is to write your cover letter. Though there may be instances where you deliver your resume in person, most often you will be sending it through the mail. Resumes sent through the mail always need an accompanying letter that briefly introduces you and your resume. The purpose of the cover letter is to get a potential employer to read your resume, just as the purpose of your resume is to get that same potential employer to call you for an interview.

Like your resume, your cover letter should be clean, neat, and direct. A cover letter usually includes the following information:

1. Your name and address (unless it already appears on your personal letterhead).

2. The date.

3. The name and address of the person and company to whom you are sending your resume.

4. The salutation ("Dear Mr." or "Dear Ms." followed by the person's last name, or "To Whom It May Concern" if you are answering a blind ad).

5. An opening paragraph explaining why you are writing (in response to an ad, the result of a previous meeting, at the suggestion of someone you both know) and indicating that you are interested in whatever job is being offered.

6. One or two more paragraphs that tell why you want to work for the company and what qualifications and experience you can bring to that company.

7. A final paragraph that closes the letter and requests that you be contacted for an interview. You may mention here that your references are available upon request.

8. The closing ("Sincerely," or "Yours Truly," followed by your signature with your name typed under it).

Your cover letter, including all of the information above, should be no more than one page in length. The language used should be polite, businesslike, and to the point. Do not attempt to tell your life story in the cover letter. A long and cluttered letter will only serve to put off the reader. Remember, you only need to mention a few of your accomplishments and skills in the cover letter. The rest of your information is in your resume. Each and every achievement should not be mentioned twice. If your cover letter is a success, your resume will be read and all pertinent information reviewed by your prospective employer.

Producing the Cover Letter

Cover letters should always be typed individually, since they are always written to particular individuals and companies. Never use a form letter for your cover letter. Cover letters cannot be copied or reproduced like resumes. Each one should be as personal as possible. Of course, once you have written and rewritten your first cover letter to the point where you are satisfied with it, you certainly can use similar wording in subsequent letters.

After you have typed your cover letter on quality bond paper, be sure to proofread it as thoroughly as you did your resume. Again, spelling errors are a sure sign of carelessness, and you don't want that to be a part of your first impression on a prospective employer. Make sure to handle the letter and resume carefully to avoid any smudges, and then mail both your cover letter and resume in an appropriate sized envelope. Be sure to keep an accurate record of all the resumes you send out and the results of each mailing, either in a separate notebook or on individual 3 × 5" index cards.

Numerous sample cover letters appear at the end of the book. Use them as models for your own cover letter or to get an idea of how cover letters are put together. Remember, every one is unique and depends on the particular circumstances of the individual writing it and the job for which he or she is applying.

Now the job of writing your resume and cover letter is complete. About a week after mailing resumes and cover letters to potential employers, you will want to contact them by telephone. Confirm that your resume arrived, and ask whether an interview might be possible. Getting your foot in the door during this call is half the battle of a job search, and a strong resume and cover letter will help you immeasurably.

Chapter Five

SAMPLE RESUMES

This chapter contains dozens of sample resumes for people pursuing a wide variety of jobs and careers.

There are many different styles of resumes in terms of graphic layout and presentation of information. These samples also represent people with varying amounts of education and experience. Use these samples to model your own resume after. Choose one resume, or borrow elements from several different resumes to help you construct your own.

AL GAMBRELL
21 BROAD ST
KANSAS CITY, MO 65443
(708)555-9354

CITY OF KANSAS CITY
Tax Analyst   1986-Present

Participated in Code 334 and 338 liquidations and asset step-ups of major corporations including formula analysis, appraisal process review, rendering legal opinion on technical issues, providing basis and earnings and profits calculations for those assets valued for tax reporting purposes in excess of $600 million.

Coordinated federal tax audit pertaining to Code 334(b) liquidation and asset value step-ups of companies. Responsibilities included sourcing units for information requests of the IRS and responding to IRS on the issues affecting properties in excess value of $200 million.

Administered pension compliance function in tax area including the filing of returns, monitoring adequacy of plan funding, and handling day to day questions. This resulted in taxes saved for over 50 plans by preserving deducibility of the pension deduction and preventing loss of a deduction for over-funding or underfunding the plan.

CARLSON AIRWAYS
Senior Tax Specialist   1984-1986

Provided research and planning assistance on legislative tax proposals and other matters including obtaining tax licenses for the sale and distribution of alcoholic beverages.

Conducted exploratory research on proposed tax legislation affecting the company and industry in general with respect to an excise tax imposed on international airfares and cargo.

Coordinated obtaining alcoholic beverage licenses following Lomas Airlines acquisition. Avoided the possibility that alcoholic beverages could not be sold or distributed on airplanes or at clubs and the penalties could be imposed.

Researched international tax treaties' impact on the international carrier to forestall imposition of foreign taxes on the carrier in new overseas operating locations.

EDUCATION: UNIVERSITY OF KANSAS
                 J.D. 1984

ALAN ARKIN
45 RIVERDALE DRIVE
RIVERMONT, FL 30887
(204)555-8294

OBJECTIVE: Attorney's position with a law firm involved in real estate, finance, environmental law, or related fields.

BACKGROUND SUMMARY: More than twenty years of experience as a corporate attorney with a major mortgage investment organization. Handled a wide variety of legal matters involving real estate financing and development, litigation and dispute management, contracts, government regulation and insurance. Additionally have been responsible for promoting the company to prospective customers and solving problems. Received the highest award in the region for outstanding job performance.

ACCOMPLISHMENTS:

MANAGEMENT AND ADMINISTRATION

Assisted in a team which created a new builder bond product and followed through with marketing the legal aspects of the new product, resulting in $5 million in commitments. Received performance award for these efforts.

Implemented procedures to control outside counsels' fees, saving $100,000 annually.

Awarded performance incentive award for writing a unique mortgage purchase commitment contract.

INVESTIGATION AND LITIGATION

Supervised major Florida litigation against fifteen corporate defendants for recovery of $2 million in losses over a two year period.

Supervised litigation to the successful end, defending the company against a $1 million wrongful death claim in Miami, without incurring a loss to our company.

Managed the legal aspects of two fraud investigations and supervised resulting litigation against two Florida lenders saving $500,000.

Supervised the defense of a $3.5 million securities fraud case to an agreed settlement.

EXPERIENCE

HOLBRECHT MANUFACTURING   1984-Present
STAFF ATTORNEY

EDUCATION

UNIVERSITY OF FLORIDA, SCHOOL OF LAW, J.D. 1984

UNIVERSITY OF MIAMI, B.A. ENGLISH, 1981

JOANNE WONG
4 SUMMIT POINTE WAY
ACTON, MI   01775   (617)   555-9988

**LEGAL
EXPERIENCE:** LACKTON & TOIL, DETROIT, MI
Summer Law Clerk: Conducted legal research and prepared legal memoranda. Attended hearings and depositions involving domestic relations issues.

UNITED STATES DEPARTMENT OF PERSONNEL
Office of the General Counsel. Drafted appellate briefs, motions, and other legal memoranda on behalf of the Secretary. Evaluated evidentiary transcripts including legal and medical documents.

EDUCATION: DETROIT UNIVERSITY SCHOOL OF LAW
Candidate for Juris Doctor Degree
   Participant in Detroit College trial advocacy program.
   First year orientation counselor
   Witness in pretrial litigation program.
   Top third of my class academically.

KANSAS STATE UNIVERSITY
B.A. Political Science & Psychology

**OTHER
EMPLOYMENT:** Retail sales clerk, health club program coordinator, and student postal clerk.

ADDITIONAL: Fluent in Spanish, English, and German. Proficient with both Macintosh and IBM computers.

ALAN JACKSONELLI
34 TUFTS LANE
NEW ORLEANS, LA   556778   806-555-2234

EDUCATION: TULANE UNIVERSITY SCHOOL OF LAW
                        Candidate for Juris Doctor degree

                        WASHINGTON UNIVERSITY
                        B.A. in Political Science & Sociology

ACTIVITIES: Law School: Moot Court Special Teams,
Finalist Fall Moot Court Competition, International Law
Society.
                        College: Selected as Campus
Representative, Washington Center for Learning Alternatives,
Treasurer South Forty Programming Board, Member Pre-Law
Society, Member Co-ed football and softball teams.

LEGAL EXPERIENCE:
                        TULANE UNIVERSITY, Research Assistant
                        Updated and researched information on
plea bargaining. Examined guidelines for judicial discretion
to determine acceptance or rejection of plea bargains.

                        WILLIAM GARDNER P.C., Paralegal
                        Prepared court documents and
interrogatories. Worked with clients through informal
interviews and discussions. Researched personAL injury and
workers' compensation claims. Organized cases and case files.

                        JAMES LAUGHLAN ESQ., Summer Intern
                        Prepared briefs, documents of custody and
client insurance forms. Investigated personal injury,
property damage, and medical malpractice claims through
trails.

OTHER EXPERIENCE:
                        SPECIAL COMMITTEE ON AGING, Intern
                        Attended Congressional hearings in areas
of interest to the Committee. Wrote memoranda. Analyzed
medical and scientific literature. Researched data from the
Library of Congress. Interviewed and prepared witnesses for
hearings.

                        MANPOWER INC., Sales Representative
                        Acted as a liaison between temporary
workers, client corporations, and employers. Interviewed
temporaries. Created organizational system for word processor
and data entry resources.

YOSHI AL BRUCHT
23 BUSTER AVE
TORRANCE, CA 90667   (207)555-7654

EDUCATION

CALIFORNIA UNIVERSITY, SCHOOL OF
LAW
J.D., MAY 1989

LACKLEE UNIVERSITY
BACHELOR OF SCIENCE DEGREE, 1985
MAJOR: ACCOUNTING

PROFESSIONAL   Certified Public Accountant

PROFESSIONAL
ASSOCIATIONS   American Institute of CPAs
California Society of CPAs
American Bar Association
Bar Association of California

EXPERIENCE   1988 TO PRESENT
Johnston Holdings

Johnston Holdings Company is a
small managed partnership which invests in
a variety of commercial ventures with an
emphasis on real estate.

Responsible for all phases of real
estate development including land
acquisition, supervision of construction
and lease negotiations.

References available uopn request

ALAN MARCUS
444 COLUMBUS DRIVE
YARDLEY, TN 67732   (204)555-7629

EDUCATION

UNIVERSITY OF TENNESSEE, SCHOOL OF LAW
J.D. 1990
Class Rank 17/223
Order of the Coif
Managing Editor, Law School Review
Scholar at Law Scholarship
Recipient of highest grade in Antitrust Law

UNIVERSITY OF THE SOUTH
B.A. Political Science
Summa Cum Laude
Studied at Imperial College, University of London

EXPERIENCE

1990 to
Present   MINORITY COUNSEL, UNITED STATES SENATE
                 COMMITTEE ON HEALTH SERVICES AND TAXATION

Recipient of the highly competitive Senator Wainwright Legal
Fellowship. Duties include proposing, drafting, and promoting
legislation for the Taxation and Health Services
Subcommittees. Emphasis has been on competition, safety, and
interstate issues and legislation.

1989   SUMMER ASSOCIATE, YOUNG & BUBLICK

Researched and drafted briefs and memoranda on anti-trust,
contract, and insurance issues. Projects included drafting a
motion for a new trial and a motion for judgment notwithstanding the verdict on an $67.5 million judgement.

1988   SUMMER ASSOCIATE, TATE, BUCK & COUGLIN

Researched and wrote on constitutional issues, including
obscenity and the ramifications of the First Amendment on
land use law.

QUAQUOE ABUGADI
23 COLGATE ST.
BUNKER NEW YORK   (207)555-9087

EDUCATION
                        HOFFSTRAW UNIVERSITY, SCHOOL OF
                        LAW
                        MASTERS OF LAW IN TAXATION
                        MAY 1989

                        LUKILEW SCHOOL OF LAW
                        J.D., MAY 1988

UNDERGRADUATE   LINSEAD UNIVERSITY
                        BACHELOR OF SCIENCE DEGREE, 1985
                        MAJOR: ACCOUNTING

PROFESSIONAL   Certified Public Accountant
                        Registered art appraiser

PROFESSIONAL
AFFILIATIONS
                        American Institute of CPAs
                        New York Society of CPAs
                        American Bar Association
                        American Real Estate Association
                        Jinka Chi Society

EXPERIENCE   1988 TO PRESENT
                        Southerby's Auction House

                        Responsible for all phases of negotiations
                        including acquisitions, deeds and contract
                        negotiations.

                        References available upon request

ALICE RANDALL
21 BROAD ST.
JACKSON, TN 65443
(708)555-9354

TENNESSEE VALLEY AUTHORITY
MANAGER OF TAX & COMPLIANCE   1986-Present

Administered pension compliance function in tax area including the filing of returns, monitoring adequacy of plan funding, and handling day-to-day questions. This resulted in taxes saved for over 50 plans.

Coordinated federal tax audit pertaining to Code 334(b) liquidation and asset value step-ups of companies. Responsibilities included sourcing units for information requests of the IRS and responding to the IRS on the issues affecting properties in excess value of $200 million.

Participated in Code 334 and 338 liquidations and asset step-ups of major corporations including formula analysis, appraisal process review, rendering legal opinion on technical issues, providing basis and earnings and profits calculations for those assets valued for tax reporting purposes in excess of $600 million.

BARWICK DEPARTMENT STORES
Senior Tax Specialist   1984-1986

Researched international tax treaties' impact on the international carrier to forestall imposition of foreign taxes on the carrier in overseas locations.

Provided research and planning assistance on legislative tax proposals and other matters including obtaining tax licenses for the sale and distribution of alcoholic beverages.

Conducted exploratory research on proposed tax legislation affecting the company and industry in general with respect to an excise tax imposed on international airfares and cargo.

EDUCATION: UNIVERSITY OF TENNESSEE
                              J.D. 1984

                              UNIVERSITY OF MISSOURI
                              B.A. ENGLISH, 1981

ARCHIE FOX
34 LAST LANE
DAYTON, OH   55678   **806-555-2234**

LEGAL EXPERIENCE:

OHIO UNIVERSITY, Research Assistant
Updated and researched information on plea bargaining. Examined guidelines for judicial discretion to determine acceptance or rejection of plea bargains.

MARK STONE P.C., Paralegal
Prepared court documents and interrogatories. Worked with clients through informal interviews and discussions. Researched person injury and workers' compensation claims. Organized cases and case files.

ALVIN EDWARDS ESQ, Summer Intern
Prepared briefs, documents of custody, and client insurance forms. Investigated personal injury, property damage, and medical malpractice claims through trials.

EDUCATION: **OHIO UNIVERSITY SCHOOL OF LAW**
Candidate for Juris Doctor degree

BOSTON UNIVERSITY
B.A. in Political Science & Sociology

ACTIVITIES: Law School: Moot Court Special Teams, Finalist Fall Moot Court Competition, International Law Society.
College: Selected as Campus Representative, Lackeley Center for Learning Alternatives, Treasurer Campus Programming Board, Member Pre-Law Society, Member Coed football and softball teams.

OTHER EXPERIENCE:

SPECIAL COMMITTEE OF CONGRESS, Intern
Attended Congressional hearings in areas of interest to the Committee. Wrote memoranda. Analyzed medical and scientific literature. Researched data from the Library of Congress. Interviewed and prepared witnesses for hearings.

TEMPO INC., Sales Representative
Acted as a liaison between temporary workers, client corporations and employers. Interviewed temporaries. Created organizational system for word processor and data entry resources.

ALYSE GOMEZ
444 YARDLEY DRIVE
ARMONG, CT   67732   **(204)555-7629**

EXPERIENCE

1990 to
Present   **ASSISTANT COUNSEL, UNITED STATES SENATE**
                     COMMITTEE ON FOOD, BEVERAGE AND HUNGER

Recipient of the highly competitive Senator Fauste Fellowship for Ethics. Duties include
proposing, drafting, and promoting legislation for the appropriate Subcommittees.
Emphasis has been on competition, safety, and interstate issues and legislation.

1989   **SUMMER ASSOCIATE, OLD & LUBLICK**

Researched and drafted briefs and memoranda on antitrust, contract, and insurance issues.
Projects included drafting a motion for a new trial and a motion for judgment
notwithstanding the verdict on an $67.5 million judgment.

1988   **SUMMER ASSOCIATE, LATE, LUCK & LOUGHLIN**

Researched and wrote on constitutional issues, including obscenity and the ramifications of
the First Amendment on land use law.

1987   **STUDENT INTERN, HOUSE OF REPRESENTATIVES**

Wrote speeches and press releases for legislators and compiled weekly legislative
summaries for statewide distribution.

EDUCATION

UNIVERSITY OF HARTFORD, SCHOOL OF LAW
J.D. 1990
Class Rank 17/223
Order of the Coif
Managing Editor, Law School Review
Scholar at Law Scholarship
Recipient of highest grade in Antitrust

UNIVERSITY OF VERMONT
B.A. Political Science
Summa Cum Laude
Studied at Imperial College, University of London

ARLENE KINGSTON
45 RIVERMONT WAY
DALLAS, TX 77230
(204)555-8294

BACKGROUND SUMMARY: Over twenty years of experience as a corporate attorney with a number of leading financial organizations. Managed a wide variety of legal matters involving real estate financing and development, litigation and dispute management, contracts, government regulation, and insurance. Additionally have been responsible for promoting the company to prospective customers and solving problems. Received the highest award in the region for outstanding job performance.

ACCOMPLISHMENTS:

ADMINISTRATION AND MANAGEMENT

Implemented procedures to control outside counsels' fees, saving $100,000 annually.

Awarded performance incentive award for writing a unique mortgage purchase commitment contract.

Assisted in a team that created a new builder bond product and followed through with marketing the legal aspects of the new product, resulting in $5 million in commitments. Received performance award for these efforts.

Developed and implemented legal guidelines for the approval for purchase of mortgages secured by leasehold estates and property subject to recreation leases resulting in keeping this market open.

INVESTIGATION AND LITIGATION

Supervised the defense of a $3.5 million securities fraud case to an agreed settlement.

Managed the legal aspects of two fraud investigations and supervised resulting litigation against two Florida lenders saving $500,000.

Supervised major multi-state litigation against fifteen corporate defendants for recovery of $2 million in losses over a two year period.

Supervised litigation to the successful end, defending the company against a $1 million wrongful death claim in Texas, without incurring a loss to our company.

Continued

ARLENE KINGSTON   Page 2

EXPERIENCE

JACKSON MANUFACTURING   1984-Present
STAFF ATTORNEY

EDUCATION

UNIVERSITY OF TEXAS, SCHOOL OF LAW, J.D. 1984

UNIVERSITY OF MAINE, B.A. ENGLISH, 1981

BARNEY SCHINEBLUME
23 ROSS WAY
DAYTON, OH 67554
(703)555-9834

CHIEF, OFFICE OF THE JUDGE ADVOCATE   1988-Present

Coordinated with local U.S. Attorney's Office on claims resulting in litigation. Drafted litigation reports detailing facts, law, recommendations, and required pleadings.

Advised for the installation of medical & dental staff on preventative law issues relating to malpractice and premises liability.

Pursued claims against tortiously liable third parties for damage and/or injury to Army property or personnel.

Served concurrently as installation magistrate deciding on propriety of search, seizure, or confinement of soldiers and searches of property on the installation.

TRAIL DEFENSE COUNSEL
U.S. Army Trial Defense   1982-1988

Represented military defendants at over 75 felony and misdemeanor trials before juries or military judge. Achieved 14 acquittals.

Negotiated numerous pretrial agreements favorable to clients.

Obtained pretrial dismissal of charges in over 55 cases.

Represented dozens of soldiers before separation tribunals and advised hundreds of clients facing non-judicial punishment action.

Selected from defense counsel Army-wide for 6-month deployment to Korea for duty with multinational peacekeeping force.

EDUCATION

YALE UNIVERSITY, SCHOOL OF LAW
J.D. Cum Laude, 1982

BOSTON UNIVERSITY
B.A. History, 1979

ABDUL ST. NORTUNG
23 ROSS WAY
CLEVELAND, OH 67554
(703)555-9834

EDUCATION

CLARKSTON COLLEGE, SCHOOL OF LAW
J.D. Degree, cum laude, 1982

CLEVELAND UNIVERSITY
B.A. History, 1979
ROTC Commander
Order of the Lambs

CHIEF, OFFICE OF THE CHIEF ADVOCATE   1988-Present

Assisted the installation magistrate in deciding on propriety of specific legal actions against soldiers and coordinated legal efforts with civilian agencies.

Pursued claims against individuals for misuse or illegal use of property or personnel.

Coordinated with local Attorney General's on legal claims by individuals. Drafted reports outlining legal alternatives and recommendations.

Consulted with medical personnel on legal issues relating to malpractice and personal liability.

DEFENSE COUNSEL   1982-1988

Selected from a candidate group of 150 officers to participate in a 16-month deployment to Russia for duty with multinational legal team.

Represented 123 US servicemen and women before legal tribunals and consulted with over 500 clients facing reprimands or other legal actions.

Represented military defendants at over 75 felony and misdemeanor trials before juries or military judge. Achieved 14 acquittals.

Negotiated numerous pretrial agreements favorable to clients.

Obtained pretrial dismissed of charges in over 55 cases.

References available upon request.

BETTYE BARNES
16 Moss Ave
Nashville, TN 55844   (807)555-9476

EDUCATION   University of Tennessee
                    J.D., 1988

                 Vanderbilt University
                    B.A., 1985
                    Majors: Psychology & Dance

EXPERIENCE

Associate   1988 to Present
Marlene, Kenneth & Marky

Proactively assist senior partners serving clients in the
consumer package goods and real estate industries. Prepare
briefs, research precedents, and interact with members of the
client's legal staff.

Play a leadership role in mentoring newly recruited staff
members and play an active role in the firm's recruitment
activities on various law school campuses.

Law Clerk
Lawrenceville Industries

Provided legal interpretations and evaluated labor and union
agreements. Researched key labor issues and drafted
appropriate documents.

Provided assistance to the corporate Counsel with general
corporate legal duties.

Customer Service Representative
Bechum Partners

Acquired insight into the customer service function and the
automotive after-market industry.

Significantly increased my proficiency in telephone
interaction with clients.

Executive Secretary/Administrative Assistant
Kidder James & Conroy

Assisted in accounting and financial projects in addition to
performing secretarial and administrative duties.

CARLOS MARCOS
45 TABOR HILL RD.
TULSA, OK 55678   (406)555-7865

EXPERIENCE
1986 to Present   MORTON ENTERPRISES
                             Vice President Law and Administration

Report to the Chairman and CEO of this multi-state holding company and
investment firm. Supervise a staff of 17 responsible for three critical
administrative company functions.

Successfully defended the company in a $23 million dollar product liability
charge, alleging unsafe manufacturing practices.

1984 to 1986   ROSSI, JAMES & PASTERNACK CPAs
                          Partner

Responsibility for managing the firm's investment banking practice. Utilized
my accounting and legal training to advise clients on financial and legal
implications of various business decisions.

Developed $45 million in new business and repeat assignments from
established clients.

1980 TO 1984   ABLE, SWAIN AND PRITCHARD
                          Partner
                          Senior Associate

Worked on legal issues affecting the financial service industry. Successfully
defended Silverman Partners in a $34 million insider trading case.

Developed seven new clients and generated $1,130,000 in new business.

EDUCATION

YALE UNIVERSITY
J.D., 1980

UNIVERSITY OF TULSA
B.S., BUSINESS, Concentration in Accounting

BOB LESTER
6 OCEAN DRIVE
WICHITA, KS 76554   (804)555-3498

EDUCATION

UNIVERSITY OF KANSAS, SCHOOL OF LAW
J.D., 1982
Editor, Banking Legal Review

UNIVERSITY OF WICHITA
B.A. POLITICAL SCIENCE, 1979
Dean's List All Semesters

CAREER SUMMARY: Creative and independent legal professional with ten years experience in corporate securities, finance, employee benefits/ERISA, and commercial transactions. Effective and efficient problem solver with superior technical competence in the following areas:

Mergers & Acquisitions	Securities & Tax Governance
SEC Reporting	Contract Negotiating
Debt/Equity Offerings	Financing Agreements
Executive Compensation	Litigation Management

EXPERIENCE

BLAKELY BANK   1982 to Present
Assistant Corporate Counsel and Corporate Attorney

Started with the bank after law school and progressed through the ranks to current position.

Organized, developed, and completed legal function of 25 mergers and acquisitions including the merger agreements, SEC and NYSE filings, shareholder meetings, blue sky requirements, due diligence, affiliate agreements, corporate trust and transmittal materials, and closing.

Organized and performed all legal functions of the corporate Secretary's office relating to the Board and its Committees and SEC and NYSE issues and filings including the annual report, annual meeting proxy statements, and Forms 10-K, 11-K and S-8. Served as sole in-house counsel on three debt shelf issues.

BOB PUPPYDALE
76 OSCAR DRIVE
OCEAN SIDE, SC 76554   (804)555-3498

SUMMARY: Creative and independent legal professional with ten years experience in corporate securities, finance, employee benefits/ERISA, and commercial transactions. Effective and efficient problem solver with superior technical competence in the following areas:

Mergers & Acquisitions	Securities & Tax Governance
SEC Reporting	Contract Negotiating
Debt/Equity Offerings	Financing Agreements
Executive Compensation	Litigation Management

OCEAN SIDE BANK   1982 to Present
Assistant Corporate Counsel and Corporate Attorney

Began with the bank after law school and progressed through the ranks to current position.

Organized, developed, and completed legal function of 25 mergers and acquisitions including the merger agreements, SEC and NYSE filings, shareholder meetings, blue sky requirements, due diligence, affiliate agreements, corporate trust, and transmittal materials and closing.

Organized and performed all legal functions of the corporate Secretary's office relating to the Board and its Committees and SEC and NYSE issues and filings including the annual report, annual meeting proxy statements, and Forms 10-K, 11-K, and S-8. Served as sole in-house counsel on three debt shelf issues.

Responsible for the legal functions relating to corporate practice, governance and insurance. Designed and executed revisions of the director and officer liability and indemnification policy.

EDUCATION

UNIVERSITY OF SOUTH CAROLINA, SCHOOL OF LAW
J.D., 1982
Editor, Banking Legal Review

UNIVERSITY OF CHARLESTON
B.A. POLITICAL SCIENCE, 1979

CARL JONES
123 WILSON AVE
CHICAGO, IL 60998
312-555-7654

NATIONAL LAUNDRIES CORPORATION   1989 to Present
Assistant Tax Manager

Supervisory responsibility for preparation and review of consolidated federal, state, local, pension, and partnership returns for over 150 companies.

Coordinated federal and state partnership and pension tax audits, fielding questions from agents or auditors and responding in a timely manner.

LAXTER COMMUNICATIONS   1982-1989
Tax Analyst

Responsible for preparation of federal, state, and local returns on consolidated and separate return basis for over 200 companies.

Researched tax questions on acquisitions, reorganizations, mergers, liquidations, and dispositions.

TWENTIETH CENTURY MOVING CORPORATION   1977-1982
Tax Analyst

Conducted tax compliance and research projects for consolidated groups of companies.

Coordinated federal tax audits, sourcing units and responding to IRS audit information requests.

EDUCATION

UNIVERSITY OF ILLINOIS, COLLEGE OF LAW
J.D. 1977

DEPAUL UNIVERSITY, SCHOOL OF BUSINESS
B.S., ACCOUNTING 1974

PROFESSIONAL AFFILIATIONS

Member of the Illinois State Bar and various Federal Courts
American Bar Association
Illinois State Bar Association
Illinois County Lawyers Association
National Association of Accountants

CARMINE JONES
123 WILSON AVE
BOSTON, MA 60998
617-555-7654

AXEL ROADS CORPORATION   1989 to Present
Assistant Tax Manager

Coordinated federal and state partnership and pension
tax audits, fielding questions from agents or auditors
and responding in a timely manner.

Supervisory responsibility for preparation and review
of consolidated federal, state, local, pension, and
partnership returns for over 150 companies.

ALSTON TELECOMMUNICATIONS   1982-1989
Tax Analyst

Researched tax questions on acquisitions,
reorganizations, mergers, liquidations, and
dispositions.

Responsible for preparation of federal, state, and
local returns on consolidated and separate return
basis for over 200 companies.

LOADSTAR INTERNATIONAL   1977-1982
Tax Analyst

Coordinated federal tax audits, sourcing units and
responding to IRS audit information requests.

Conducted tax compliance and research projects for
consolidated groups of companies.

Continued on next page

CARMINE JONES   **Page 2**

EDUCATION

UNIVERSITY OF BOSTON, COLLEGE OF LAW
J.D. 1977

LEDLERLY UNIVERSITY, SCHOOL OF BUSINESS
B.S., ACCOUNTING 1974

PROFESSIONAL AFFILIATIONS

Member of the MA State Bar and various Federal Courts
American Bar Association
MA State Bar Association
MA County Lawyers Association
National Association of Accountants

SARAH GORMAN
3716 MACLOUD
NEW ORLEANS, LA   66778   **(907)555-5632**

OBJECTIVE: Seeking a position as a law firm associate that would utilize my background and legal training.

EDUCATION   Clarkston University Law School
                                 Juris Doctor 1988
                                 Class Rank Top Third

                                 Master of Science History
                                 Western State University, 1985
                                 GPA   3.85/4.0

                                 B.A. History, 1984
                                 Lomax State University
                                 GPA   3.4/4.0

EXPERIENCE   Corrections Legal Staff   1988-Present
                                 Department of Justice
                                 Board of Probation & Parole

Served as legal liaison with more than 15 federal and local law enforcement parties.

Appeared in court more than 120 times to testify and dispose witnesses on drug and criminal mischief cases

Skilled in fraud detection techniques.

Interviewed and obtained depositions from family members and employers in a timely and efficient manner.

Expert knowledge of the rules as they apply to precedent.

Authored memo's tot he chief of staff, reviewed information from correctional facilities and community resources.

Coordinated local efforts with social agencies and community resources.

                                 Legislative Intern
                                 Representative Martinez Gonzalez   1987-1988

Researched and filed key legislative bills.

Attended bill hearings.

References available upon request

GEORGE SUSSMAN
3716 MALLARD
BOSTON, MA 01994   (617)555-5632

OBJECTIVE: Seeking a position as a law firm associate that would utilize my background and legal training.

EDUCATION   Boston University Law School
                           Juris Doctor 1989
                           Class Rank 112/215

                           Master of Science-Criminal Justice
                           Massachusetts State University, 1986
                           GPA 3.85/4.0

                           B.A. Criminal Justice, 1985
                           Plymouth State University
                           GPA 3.4/4.0

EXPERIENCE   Criminal Justice Legal Staff 1989-Present
                           Department of Corrections

Counseled clients to stabilize problem areas.

Coordinated efforts with social agencies and community resources.

Expert knowledge of legal precedents as they apply to probation and parole.

Authored reports. reviewed information from treatment facilities and community resources.

Served as legal liaison for the Courts and Board.

Appeared in court more than 35 times to testify and dispose witnesses on a variety of case materials.

Skilled in appropriate investigative techniques.

Interviewed and obtained depositions from clients, police, family members, and employers in a timely and efficient manner.

IRENE MARCOS
45 TILLY RD.
HOUSTON, TX   55678   **(406)555-7865**

EXPERIENCE
1986 to Present   **C.F. CONSTRUCTION**
                              Vice President Finance, Law, and Administration

Report to the Chairman and CEO of this multi-state real estate construction firm. Supervise a staff of 27 responsible for three critical company functions.

Successfully defended the company in a multimillion dollar EEOC charge, alleging unfair hiring practices. Won case on appeal in the third district court.

1984 to 1986   **PAUL R. MARTIN CPAs**
                              Partner

Overall responsibility for guiding and managing the firm's construction industry practice. Utilized my accounting and legal training to advise clients on financial and legal implications of various business decisions.

Developed $45 million in new business and repeat assignments from established clients.

1980 to 1984   **WANBURG, YOUNG AND CRICHTON**
                              Partner
                              Senior Associate
                              Associate

Worked on complex legal issues affecting the construction industry. Served clients in the Southwest and Midwest regions of the United States. Successfully defended Crain Construction in a $34 million wrongful damage case.

Article published in U.S. Lawyer Magazine on legal issues impacting the construction industry, generated new billings in excess of $76,000.

EDUCATION

HARVARD UNIVERSITY
J.D., 1980

UNIVERSITY OF ILLINOIS
B.S., BUSINESS, Concentration in Accounting

Admitted to the Texas, Missouri, and Louisiana Bars.

JACK REISENBERG
10 TOMCAT LANE
SAN FRANCISCO, CA 98432
(907)555-7622

OBJECTIVE: A management level position in a tax department or tax attorney with specialization in research, planning, analysis, and compliance.

SUMMARY: Tax attorney with over 15 years of diverse management level responsibilities in the corporate tax department. Project level responsibilities include:

Extensive work in 334/338 corporate liquidations and asset value step-ups.

Research and planning with respect to legislation in the tax area.

Position papers addressing management's tax concerns and IRS audit information requests.

Basis and earnings and profits calculations for sales and dispositions of various assets.

Commentary review on license agreements, acquisitions. re-organizations, mergers, liquidations, and other dispositions.

Compliance level responsibilities in tax areas dictated by legal or international ramifications.

EDUCATION: STANFORD UNIVERSITY, SCHOOL OF LAW
J.D. 1976

YALE UNIVERSITY
B.S., MECHANICAL ENGINEERING, 1973

EXPERIENCE:

ASHLAND ENGINEERING AND CONSTRUCTION
Tax Director   1976-Present

Administered foreign sales compliance function for engineering group including contract review, foreign funds sweeps, estimated taxes, monitoring flow through of FSC benefits to source which provided units with $500,000 in tax benefits.

Coordinated California tax audit for an audit period in excess of ten years which included sourcing units for information requests and responding to an auditor on those requests, sustaining use of the non-unitary tax treatment and resulting in a $300,000 reduction to a proposed assessment in a subsequent audit period.

Administered boycott program for tax reporting purposes including questionnaire presentation and unit sourcing, interpreting and disclosing boycott reportable activity which provided a monitoring device for over 200 companies where tax benefits could otherwise be lost and penalties imposed.

JAMES CHANG
2 SABOR AVENUE
JACKSON, NEBRASKA 33456
(765)555-8943

EDUCATION

University of Nebraska, College of Law
J.D. 1989
Class Rank, Top Third
Honors & Activities
     Iowa Law Reviews
     Clinical Law Program
     Phi Delta Phi
     Graduated with Distinction

University of Alabama
B.S. Business Administration, 1986
Class rank: Top 15%
Honors & Activities
     Society for Management
     Student Government-Treasurer
     Beta Gamma Sigma Award
     Graduated with High Honors

PROFESSIONAL
EXPERIENCE

1989 to Present

Young & Daulston
Associate

General civil, insurance, and corporate litigation. Engage in motion and trial practice, draft pleadings, take depositions, and conduct other discovery activities.

1988

Lucklee & Chambliss
Law Clerk

Attended and assisted civil and criminal hearings and trials. Researched and prepared memoranda in areas such as corporate, contract, and administrative law.

JAMIL RAI
5 LUBOR AVENUE
WICHITA, KS 98445
(765)555-0855

EDUCATION

University of Iowa, College of Law
J.D. 1988
Class Rank, Top Half
Honors & Activities
    Law Reviews
    Criminal Law Program
    Chi Fi Die
    Graduated with Honors

University of Maine
B.S. Business Administration, 1985
Class rank: Top 35%
Honors & Activities
    Society for Business
    Student Government-VP Finance
    Phi Holo Tau Award
    Graduated with Honors

PROFESSIONAL EXPERIENCE

1988 to Present   **Long & Long**
        Associate

Work in the areas of civil, insurance and corporate litigation. Assist in motion and trial practice. Additionally, am responsible for developing initial draft pleadings and other discovery activities.

1988   **Hatless & Gore**
    Clerk

Participated in civil and criminal hearings and trials. Assisted senior partners in research and preparing memoranda. Primary focus was in the fields of corporate, contract and administrative law.

JANET CORBIN
23 KINGS WAY
LOS ANGELES, CA 98334   (510)555-4893

WELLS FARGO BANK
ATTORNEY   1987 to Present

Negotiated and wrote term and revolving credit agreements,
loan participation agreements, corporate and consumer loan
documents, equipment leases, computer equipment contracts,
software licenses, and computer service agreements.

Performed regulatory analysis on pending local, state, and
federal legislation.

Performed special projects on regulatory and contract
compliance analysis of Risk Management and Insurance
Department and company employee stores.

Advised Human Resources Division on employment law issues.

CRIMINAL JURY INSTRUCTIONS COMMITTEE
RESEARCH ASSISTANT TO CHIEF REPORTER   1985-1987

MATTHEW BENDER & CO.
CRIMINAL LAW EDITOR   1984-1985

LEGAL AID SOCIETY
ATTORNEY   1983-1984

SHERMAN & BULLION
ATTORNEY   1980-1983

EDUCATION

J.D., UCLA, International Law Fellowship, 1980

MBA, USC, Major in Finance, 1977

B.A., UCLA, Major in Religion, 1975

Admission: California Bar

PROFESSIONAL ACTIVITIES

President of Corporate Counsel Association of Greater Los
Angeles

Member of Electronic Fund Transfer Subcommittee of American
Bar Association

JANET JACKSON
10 LUCKY LANE
LOS ANGELES CA 98432
(907)555-7622

OBJECTIVE: A management level position as a tax attorney with specialization in research, planning, analysis and compliance.

SUMMARY: Tax attorney with over 10 years of diverse management level responsibilities in the corporate tax department. Project level responsibilities include:

Commentary review on license agreements, acquisitions. reorganizations, mergers, liquidations, and other dispositions.

Compliance level responsibilities in tax areas dictated by legal or international ramifications.

Extensive work in 334/338 corporate liquidations and asset value step-ups.

Research and planning with respect to legislation in the tax area.

Position papers addressing management's tax concerns and IRS audit information requests.

Basis and earnings and profits calculations for sales and dispositions of various assets.

EDUCATION: LACKLAND UNIVERSITY, SCHOOL OF LAW
                        J.D. 1976

                        MUSTON UNIVERSITY
                        B.S., MECHANICAL ENGINEERING, 1973

EXPERIENCE:

Townsend Operations Inc.
Tax Director

Administered boycott program for tax reporting purposes including questionnaire presentation and unit sourcing, interpreting and disclosing boycott reportable activity which provided a monitoring device for over 200 companies where tax benefits could otherwise be lost and penalties imposed.

Continued

JANET JACKSON   Page 2

Administered foreign sales compliance function for engineering group including contract review, foreign funds sweeps, estimated taxes, monitoring flow through of FSC benefits to source which provided units with $500,000 in tax benefits.

Coordinated California tax audit for an audit period in excess of ten years which included sourcing units for information requests and responding to an auditor on those requests, sustaining use of the non-unitary tax treatment and resulting in a $300,000 reduction to a proposed assessment in a subsequent audit period.

References available upon request.

JANICE MARTINEZ
23 WATERS ST
BALTIMORE, MD 55676
(304)555-7622

EXPERIENCE: CORPORATE TAX ACCOUNTANT
                     Baltimore Federal 1990 to Present

Calculated and filed monthly, quarterly, and annual
sales and use tax returns for domestic headquarters of
an international company. Performed internal audit of
company headquarters and presented final report and
recommendations to department heads.

                     AUTO CLAIM REPRESENTATIVE
                     State Farm Insurance

Established files concerning customer claims. Assessed
value of customer loss and referred file to proper
party for review. Worked 25 hours per week while in
law school to assist in financing legal education.

                     LEGAL SECRETARY
                     Harold Cooney Esq.

Processed legal documents for acquisition and sale of
real estate. Ordered title searches. Processed and
witnessed legal documents for trusts and wills.
Performed general office duties while in first year of
law school.

EDUCATION: LINCOLN UNIVERSITY
                     SCHOOL OF LAW
                     MASTERS OF LAW IN TAXATION
                     L.L.M., 1990

                     HOOVER UNIVERSITY
                     SCHOOL OF LAW
                     J.D., 1989

                     KENNEDY UNIVERSITY
                     B.A. HISTORY

PERSONAL: Computer literate in LEXIS,
WESTLAW, Basic, Lotus 1-2-3, Microsoft Word,
WordPerfect. Interests include tennis, jogging,
swimming, reading, and solving word puzzles.

JASON PATRICK
23 VERO BEACH BLVD.
MAITLAND, FL 55632   (607)555-7322

SUMMARY: A versatile business lawyer with broad legal
and management expertise in corporate, financial,
regulatory, and environmental matters. Strong
demonstrated interpersonal skills in a variety of
legal and management situations.

EMPLOYMENT EXPERIENCE

TETON CORPORATION   1979- Present
A Fortune 1000 company engaged in the chemical and
synthetic fiber industries. Annual revenues of $2.8
billion and approximately 1,200 employees.

EXECUTIVE VICE PRESIDENT-FINANCE, LAW & ADMINISTRATION
1987-Present

GENERAL COUNSEL   1985-1987
ASSISTANT GENERAL COUNSEL   1979-1985
MEMBER OF BOARD OF DIRECTORS   1988-PRESENT

ACCOMPLISHMENTS

Guided the company through a three-year out-of-court
workout with its nineteen-member bank group and other
creditors. Activities included numerous renegotiations
of credit agreements, bankruptcy contingency planning,
asset sales including refineries, crude chemical
reserves, real estate, and miscellaneous businesses.
Additionally, responsible for reduction of corporate
overhead and preservation of tax loss carry-forwards.

Led successful refinancing of company through a public
sale of $56 million of bonds and preferred stock. Made
presentations to groups and individuals.

Negotiated more than 25 major working capital facility
agreements.

Prepared more than 75 SEC filings, including
registration and proxy statements and annual/quarterly
reports. Counseled board and management on a variety
of security law matters including disclosure and
insider-trading issues.

Continued

JASON PATRICK   **Page 2**

EDUCATION

L.L.M.   **(TAX) UNIVERSITY OF FLORIDA**   **1979**

J.D.,   **UNIVERSITY OF MIAMI**   **1977**

B.A.   **HISTORY, WAYNE STATE UNIVERSITY**   **1974**

JIM KAPOWSKI
23 HUSON ST.
JACKSON, MD 55876
(304)555-4422

EXPERIENCE: CORPORATE ATTORNEY & TAX ACCOUNTANT
        Mogul Enterprises 1990 to Present

Performed internal audit of company headquarters and presented final report
and recommendations to department heads. Calculated and filed monthly,
quarterly, and annual sales and use tax returns for domestic headquarters of
an international company.

        CUSTOMER SERVICE AGENT
        Balmar Associates

Worked 25 hours per week while in law school to assist in financing legal
education. Established files concerning customer claims. Assessed value of
customer loss and referred file to proper party for review.

        ADMINISTRATIVE ASSISTANT
        Tim Lane Esq.

Performed general office duties while in first year of law school. Processed
legal documents for acquisition and sale of real estate. Ordered title searches.
Processed and witnessed legal documents for trusts and wills.

EDUCATION   AGNEW UNIVERSITY
        SCHOOL OF LAW
        MASTERS OF LAW IN TAXATION
        L.L.M., 1990

        BARNWELL UNIVERSITY
        SCHOOL OF LAW
        J.D., 1989

        NORWICH UNIVERSITY
        B.A. HISTORY

References available upon request

JOHN CORBET
32 ALWAYS WAY
SAN FRANCISCO, CA 98334   (510)555-4893

EDUCATION

J.D., UCLA, International Law Fellowship, 1980

M.B.A, USC, Major in Finance, 1977

B.A., UCLA, Major in Religion, 1975

Admission: California Bar

CALIFORNIA FIDELITY BANK
ATTORNEY   1987 to Present

Performed special projects on regulatory and contract compliance analysis of Risk Management and Insurance Department and company employee stores.

Advised Human Resources Division on employment law issues.

Negotiated and wrote term and revolving credit agreements, loan participation agreements, corporate and consumer loan documents, equipment leases, computer equipment contracts, software licenses, and computer service agreements.

Performed regulatory analysis on pending local, state, and federal legislation.

CRIMINAL JURY INSTRUCTIONS COMMITTEE
RESEARCH ASSISTANT TO CHIEF REPORTER   1985-1987

JASON LAYLER & CO
CRIMINAL LAW EDITOR   1984-1985

LEGAL AID OF CALIFORNIA
ATTORNEY   1983-1984

JACKSON & SONER
ATTORNEY   1980-1983

References available upon request

JOHN LINCONI
87 GREMLIN PLACE
VOLSBURG, MD 21066
(978)654-0933

EDUCATION:

UNIVERSITY OF LOUISVILLE COLLEGE OF LAW
J.D. May 1987
Admissions Editor, Louisville Law Journal

WASHINGTON TECH UNIVERSITY
B.A. Math, 1984
Cum Laude
Senior Research Fellow, Department of Mathematics
Cadet Commander, Reserve Officers Training Corps Detachment
Samuel Marshall Scholar
Who's Who Among American Scholars, ROTC, Student Government
Varsity Football

PROFESSIONAL EXPERIENCE:

SENIOR ATTORNEY, OFFICE OF GENERAL COUNSEL
CENTRAL INTELLIGENCE AGENCY   1991 to Present

Devise litigation and discovery strategies.

Serve as lead Agency counsel in a variety of classified prosecution cases Involving U.S. interests overseas. Coordinate legal activities between the CIA and the National Security Agency (NSA).

Manage and monitor assignments of primary federal tort and criminal litigation involving CIA or CIA interests.

Represent the Agency before the Equal Employment Opportunity Commission, the Department of Justice, and other executive departments and before judicial bodies.

Provide administrative law advice and opinions and administer the C.I.A.'s claims program.

ATTORNEY, CLAIMS BRANCH, OFFICE OF THE STAFF JUDGE ADVOCATE
Headquarters, 4TH Light Infantry   1987-1991

Investigated federal tort claims filed against the U.S. Army totalling over $312 million.

In charge of adjudicating over 1,000 federal claims per year involving over $30 million.

References provided upon request

LAMAR JONES
5 MASON RD.
DAYTON, OHIO 67885   (984)555-9254

EXPERIENCE   Carson & McMann P.C.
                        Associate   1988-Present

Conduct witness interviews, prepare trial briefs, legal memoranda, and
deposition summaries. Responsible for filings in state and federal courts.
Emphasis in criminal law and various areas of civil law.

                        Jackson Home Health Systems
                        Legal Intern 1987

Prepared legal documents and forms. Researched health law and corporate
issues. Attended various hospital committee meetings.

                        Honorable April May
                        United States Superior Judge
                        Legal Intern 1987

Drafted orders and Reports and Recommendations in district court. Extensive
research involving civil rights and petitions for habeas corpus.

                        Bob Miles, Esquire
                        Summer Associate 1986

Extensive research in the area of insurance defense and products liability for
80 attorney firm. Prepared trial briefs, legal memoranda, and drafted
interrogatories. Attended depositions and prepared deposition summaries.

                        Honorable Sarah Lee
                        Superior Court of Marsdon County
                        Legal Intern 1986

Researched in civil law with emphasis on health insurance. Drafted letter
opinions and prepared judicial orders.

Continued

LAMAR JONES   Page 2

Superior Court of Apple County
Court Clerk 1985

Assisted judges and worked in administrative offices. Responsible for all administrative functions and maintenance of court records. Gained extensive courtroom exposure in the various courts and had continual interaction with judges, attorneys, and clients.

EDUCATION   Ohio State University, School of Law
                        Juris Doctorate, 1988
                        Top 30 percent

                        Vanderbilt University
                        Bachelor of Arts: Psychology, 1985
                        Dean's List
                        Alpha Chi Omega Sorority

References provided upon request

LANCE JACOBSON
1243 PRINCE ROAD
ARLINGTON, VA   87554
(508)555-8834

OBJECTIVE: A senior Human Resources management position which would effectively utilize my experience and legal education.

EMPLOYERS: **YOUNG & BARKLEY INTERNATIONAL   1990-Present**
Corporate Manager, Human Resources Department

GENERAL DYNAMICS   1985-1990
Manager Human Resources

EXPERTISE:
EMPLOYMENT, STAFFING & EEO

Experience in managing the employment, staffing and EEO functions.
Planned, developed, and implement, several EEO initiative that increased the company's visibility among minority groups and women.
Successfully screened, interviewed, tested, and recruited both exempt and non-exempt personnel.
Responsible for the successful introduction of the company's relocation policy.
Developed alliances with professional recruiters, advertising agencies, and temporary services.
Designed and implemented job posting programs.
Authored affirmative action plans and policies.
Successfully defended employers against charges of discrimination.

EDUCATION: **CALIFORNIA STATE COLLEGE OF LAW**
J.D. 1985

UNIVERSITY OF SOUTHERN CALIFORNIA
B.A. BUSINESS ADMINISTRATION
Minor in Sociology

LARRY MCGRATH
12 HALF MOON DRIVE
PORTLAND, OR   34221   (607)555-6677

EDUCATION: University of Portland, School of Law
                                J.D. 1989

                                Southwest Missouri State University
                                B.S. Accounting, 1980
                                Captain, ROTC

EXPERIENCE: LEGAL SERVICES OF PORTLAND
1990-present   Attorney

Interviewed, counseled, and corresponded with clients primarily in
consumer areas including truth in lending, fraud, and buyer
transactions. Conducted extensive research. Additionally represent
mental patients in civil and administrative disputes.

1989-1990   COMPTON LEGAL SERVICES
                                Attorney

Drafted motions and pleadings. Researched memos for supervising
attorney. Represented several clients at informal hearings. Cases
involved housing and bankruptcy.

1982-1986   UNITED STATES ARMY
                                FT. HOOD, TEXAS
                                Training Resource Manager

Provided training to the saff offices of the 23rd Signal Brigade, a
unit of 2,200 personnel. Forecasted, allotted, and scheduled land
and training resource requirements. Designed and organized an in-
house records system. Wrote several sections of an Army "how-to"
manual. Awarded Army Commendation Medal.

1980-1982   RADIO SHACK
                                Computer Salesperson

Sold and supported Tandy computer hardware, peripherals, and
popular software packages.

References available upon request

LARRY CHANG
4 OAK DRIVE
WESTWOOD, OH 33485
(908)555-8834

OBJECTIVE: A position in Human Resources which would effectively utilize my legal training and related expertise. Particular strengths in EEO, labor, staffing, and compensation.

EMPLOYERS:
Hoffman Manufacturing   1990-Present
Director of Human Resources

Alstron Aerospace   1985-1990
Manager Human Resources
Staff Attorney

EXPERTISE:

COMPENSATION & BENEFITS

Experience in management of the compensation and benefits functions.
Performed evaluations, job analysis, and prepared job descriptions.
Developed and utilized salary surveys.

STAFFING & EEO

Designed and implemented job posting programs.
Authored affirmative action plans and policies.
Successfully defended employers against charges of discrimination.
Trained supervisors in areas of employment law and EEO
Experience in managing the employment, staffing and EEO functions.
Planned, developed, and implemented several EEO initiative that increased the company's visibility among minority groups and women.
Successfully screened, interviewed, tested, and recruited both exempt and non-exempt personnel.
Responsible for the successful introduction of the company's relocation policy.
Developed alliances with professional recruiters, advertising agencies, and temporary services.

EDUCATION:
OHIO STATE COLLEGE OF LAW
J.D. 1985

UNIVERSITY OF MASSACHUSETTS
B.A. English
Minor in French

LATIMER SCHWARTZ
67 CLEVELAND RD.
NEW YORK, NY   10223
212-555-7843

CORPORATE COUNSEL   1986   to   Present
INSURANCE SYSTEMS OF THE UNITED STATES

Responsible for all corporate and regulatory legal work for start-up subsidiary. Additionally, responsible for negotiating major computer software licenses and development contracts with corporate customers.

Hired by the firm as a result of legal and business advice rendered while at Queen & Knokic.

Awarded sales incentive trip as result of assistance in closing new business in first six months on the job.

ATTORNEY   **1982-1986**
QUEEN & KNOKIC

Hired as walk-on at premier New York law firm.

Designed innovative capital structure for $8.76 million private placement used to start new ventures.

EDUCATION:

UNIVERSITY OF NEW YORK, SCHOOL OF LAW
J.D.   1980

SUNY-BUFFALO
B.A. ENGLISH 1974

References   available   upon   request

LESTER MARTIN
2 BUNCH PALMS
DELMAR, MO 67554
(314)555-8486

EDUCATION:

Legal   Washington University, School of Law, May 1992
             Graduated 6 of 192, GPA 92.08

             Order of the Coif
             Executive Notes Editor, Washington Law Quarterly
             First Place ABA Moot Court Regional Competition
             Golden Quill Award Winner, Rutledge Moot Court Competition
             Author, Due Process on the Power of U.S. Courts to Try Foreign
             Nationals

College   University of Kansas, May 1986
             Graduated with High Distinction-GPA 3.94
             Major: Political Science, Minors: English & History

WORK EXPERIENCE:

THE HONORABLE WILLIAM BARNSTABLE   **1993-Present**
Law Clerk

Responsible for researching and writing orders in response to written motions
as well as aiding in instruction conferences and resolution of evidentiary
matters arising during civil and criminal trials.

THE HONORABLE BRUCE THOMAS   **1992-1993**
Law Clerk

Responsible for writing memoranda and draft opinions for cases pending before
the state's highest court based upon oral arguments, briefs of counsel, and
independent legal research. Additionally responsible for drafting rules for
regulatory bodies under the Court's jurisdiction.

SHERLOCK, GRAVES & AGGASSI   **Summer 1991**
Summer Associate

Engaged in research of various legal issues with responsibility for preparing
memoranda, motions, briefs, and corporate documents.

ALBERT, JONES & ACORN   **Summer 1990**
Summer Associate

Engaged in research and writing of memoranda, motions, briefs, discovery
documents, and client correspondence.

LINDA SINK
144 WALTHAM ROAD
SAN DIEGO, CA 90665   (607)555-6677

EDUCATION: University of San Diego, School of Law
                           J.D. 1989

                           California State University
                           B.S. Accounting, 1980
                           Captain, NROTC

EXPERIENCE: SUMMERS & WHITE
1990-present   Attorney

Represent indigent patients in civil and administrative disputes. Interview,
counsel, and correspond with clients primarily in consumer areas including
truth in lending, fraud, and buyer transactions. Conduct extensive research.

1989-1990   DOALSTON & TULL
                           Attorney

Drafted motions and pleadings. Researched memos for supervising attorney.
Represented several clients at informal hearings. Cases involved housing and
bankruptcy.

1982-1986   UNITED STATES NAVY
                           U.S.S. ENTERPRISE
                           Logistics Manager

Serve as logistic manager for the staff offices of the 7th fleet, a unit with 300
personnel. Forecasted, allotted and scheduled land and training resource
requirements. Designed and organized an in-house records system. Wrote
several sections of a Navy logistics manual. Awarded Navy Commendation
Medal.

1980-1982   CARLTON COMPUTER
                           Computer Salesperson

Sold and supported IBM computer hardware, peripherals, and popular
software packages.

LONNIE AMES
34 AKRON RD
MAITLAND, FL 22343
607-555-7843

CORPORATE CHIEF COUNSEL   1986 to Present
WORLD WIDE WIDGET

Recruited to the firm as a result of the quality of legal and business advice provided when at Tuck & Amos.

Responsible for all corporate and regulatory legal work for a start-up division involved in the exportation and marketing of titanium widgets used by the trucking industry. Also was responsible for negotiating major user software licenses and material contracts with corporate customers.

Achieved 115% of bonus target as a result of superior work on the new division's business in first six months on the job.

ATTORNEY   1980-1986
TUCK & AMOS

First recent law school graduate hired by the firm in three years.

Designed innovative financial lease buy-back for $8 million capitalization used to start new ventures.

EDUCATION:

UNIVERSITY OF FLORIDA, SCHOOL OF LAW
J.D. 1980

COLLEGE OF ST. MARY'S
B.A. ENGLISH 1974

OTHER EXPERIENCE

Prior to returning to law school, played professional baseball for the AA club of the Kansas City Royal's organization.

LOUIS JONES
56 LEMEY DRIVE
BELMONT, MA 09887
(617)555-8486

EDUCATION:

Legal   Harvard University, School of Law, May 1992
           Graduated 44 of 192, GPA 90.08

           Order of the Coif
           Executive Quality Editor, Harvard Law Quarterly
           First Place Moot Court Division Competition
           Silver Quill Award Winner, Longstreet Moot Court Competition
           Author, Due Process of U.S. Courts to Import Silver from Cuba

           University of Boston, May 1986
           Graduated with Distinction-GPA 3.74
           Major: Political Science, Minors: English & History

WORK EXPERIENCE:

THE HONORABLE FREDERICK RUBLE   1993-Present
Law Clerk

Responsible for writing memoranda and draft opinions for cases pending before the state's
highest court based upon oral arguments, briefs of counsel and independent legal research.
Additionally responsible for drafting rules for regulatory bodies under the Court's jurisdiction.

THE HONORABLE BERNARD WILMER JR.   1992-1993
Law Clerk

Responsible for researching and writing orders in response to written motions as well as aiding in
instruction conferences and resolution of evidentiary matters arising during civil and criminal trials.

BECKER, MOYNAHAN & SCHULTZ   Summer 1991
Summer Associate

Engaged in research of various legal issues with responsibility for preparing memoranda, motions,
briefs, and corporate documents.

EDDY, EBB & LISA   Summer 1990
Summer Associate

Engaged in research and writing of memoranda, motions, briefs, discovery documents, and client
correspondence.

MARC EDMONBROSHIAN
3 WEST PLACE
ST. LOUIS, MO   63001
314-555-8765

EDUCATION   J.D., WASHINGTON UNIVERSITY
                             SCHOOL OF LAW, 1988
                             Member of Environmental Law Society
                             Member of Phi Delta Phi Legal Fraternity

                             B.A., HORTON COLLEGE, 1984
                             Major: Medieval History
                             GPA 3.6/4.0
                             Founder, Coalition for Responsible
                             Investments
                             Graduated with High Honors

EXPERIENCE

ATTORNEY, Self Employed, 1990-Present

Presently contract with several practitioners to do research and
writing work on a variety of Employment Law issues and cases.

ATTORNEY, Legal Services of St. Louis, 1988-1990

Handled all aspects of client's case except court appearances.
Work included initial interviews, all subsequent client contact, and
the writing of memoranda, briefs, and a variety of motions.
Generally handled 10-15 clients at a time. Practice focused on
consumer-contract law.

JUDICIAL INTERN, The Honorable Nathan Nance, Magistrate of the
United States District Court for the Eastern District of Missouri.
Summer 1987

Conducted research and wrote memoranda on a variety of motions.

WRITER, 20th Century Fox Film Corporation, 1984-1985

Worked on the development of the first draft for the film They All
Came Running." Developed plot synopsis and incorporated
changes at the behest of the film's director H. Martin Smith. Film
was released in the summer of 1988 starring Ellen Thomas and
Hugh Young.

MARY MCGRATH
12 OAK DR.
JACKSON, TN 44559   (607)555-2345

EDUCATION   UNIVERSITY OF TENNESSEE
                   Candidate for Juris Doctor Degree
                   Honors: Executive Editorial Board and Business Manager
of the Business Developments Journal; Member of the Moot Court Society

                   VANDERBILT UNIVERSITY
                   Bachelor of Arts, Major in English

                   CITY OF MUNICH EXTENSION
                   Study Abroad, Interdisciplinary

PUBLICATIONS   BUSINESS DEVELOPMENTS JOURNAL:Authored article
entitled "Recent Developments in Business Development Law, Legal Implications
of Tax Deferred Financing."

ACTIVITIES   LAW SCHOOL-LITP Program Participant, Student Legal
Services, Tax Preparer for Social Responsibility Program, Member Law Society,
Student Advisor to incoming law students.

LEGAL
EXPERIENCE   DISTRICT ATTORNEY'S OFFICE
                   Legal Internship: Active involvement in all aspects of the
prosecutor's office pursuant to Tennessee Third Year Practice Act. Courtroom
experience and involvement in plea negotiations and drafting of indictments and
trial briefs.

                   JILLIAN & SMOOT
                   Summer Associate: Researched and wrote legal briefs.
Filed motion papers and memoranda in real estate, labor, employment
discrimination, and negligence cases. Assisted in closings, digested depositions, and
attended pretrial conferences.

                   CHIEF JUDGE ALLAN NOTHINGS, UNITED STATES
FEDERAL COURT OF APPEAL
                   Judicial Clerkship: Researched and drafted opinions on
bankruptcy cases and proceedings. Acted as Courtroom Deputy and observed
adversary proceedings, motion practices, and key meetings.

MARK RASTAI
34 BIRCH DRIVE
GREELEY, CT   56778

(903)555-3925

EDUCATION

University of Connecticut
J.D. 1990
Student Legal Advisors
New England Law Society

University of Rhode Island
Bachelor of Arts in English, 1987
National Honor Society
Beta Phi Scholarship Committee

University of France
Completed study abroad program, 1986

EXPERIENCE

LASTER, MORELAND & HUNG
ASSOCIATE

Admitted to the Massachusetts and Connecticut State Bars.

Served on a firm task force to increase billing efficiencies through automation. Assisted in the drafting of a proposal to senior partners which was later adopted by the firm.

Conduct research in support of the senior partner in charge of the firm's real estate industry practice.

File motions with the county clerk's office and provide administrative support as needed.

NON-LEGAL EXPERIENCE

City of Chancey
County Clerk

Organized instructional programs geared toward senior citizens which incorporated financial, real estate, and management subjects.

MARK STALL
465 A POINTE WAY
LASTLEY, OR 01775   (617) 555-9988

LEGAL
EXPERIENCE: DARTON, GLARM & GORSTON, PORTLAND, OR
                               Summer Law Clerk: Conducted legal research and
prepared legal memoranda. Attended hearings and depositions involving
domestic relations issues.

                               OREGON DEPT. OF PERSONNEL
                               Office of the General Counsel. Drafted appellate
briefs, motions and other legal memoranda on behalf of the Secretary.
Evaluated evidentiary transcripts including legal and medical documents.

EDUCATION: OREGON UNIVERSITY SCHOOL OF LAW
                               Candidate for Juris Doctor Degree
                                     Participant in Detroit College trial
                               advocacy program.
                                     First year orientation counselor
                                     Witness in pretrial litigation
                               program.
                                     Top third of my class academically.

                               TEXAS STATE UNIVERSITY
                               B.A. Political Science & Psychology

OTHER
EMPLOYMENT: Retail sales clerk, health club program
                               coordinator, and student postal clerk.

ADDITIONAL: Fluent in Spanish, English, and German.
                               Proficient with both Macintosh and IBM
                               computers.

References are available upon request

```
MARSTAND RUBBLE JR.
324 OAK DRIVE
LINCOLN, UTAH   56778                    (903)555-3925
```

EDUCATION   University of Utah
J.D. 1990
Student Legal Services
International Law Society

University of North Carolina
Bachelor of Arts in History, 1987
Golden Key National Honor Society
Phi Delta Scholarship Committee

University of London
Completed study abroad program, 1986

EXPERIENCE   HOBSON, CLAVIN & BING
ASSOCIATE

Conduct research in support of the senior partner in charge of the firm's construction industry practice.

File motions with the county clerk's office and provide administrative support as needed.

Admitted to the Utah and New Mexico State Bars.

Served on a firm task force to increase billing efficiency through automation. Assisted in the drafting of a proposal to senior partners which was later adopted by the firm.

NON-LEGAL EXPERIENCE

CITY OF MELBOURNE
Swimming Instructor

Organized swimming instruction programs that incorporated swimming, diving, and safety skills. Instructed and certified children between the ages of two and fourteen.

MARCIE WEINBERG
21 LANCE PKWY.
NEW ROCHELLE, NY 09556   607-555-7622

EMPLOYMENT BACKGROUND

1988 to Present   Long & Adler
                                 Associate

Researched various areas of law including Bankruptcy, Labor/Employment
and Commercial Litigation. General practice firm comprised of approximately
100 attorneys.

1985 to 1988   Larson & Upton
                                 Associate

Researched various areas of law including Environmental Law, Bankruptcy
Law and Commercial Transactions. General practice firm comprised of
approximately 230 attorneys.

1984-1985   The Honorable Anne Pettingell
                                 United States District Judge
                                 Law Clerk

Researched precedents and opinions in support of Chambers. Discussed
precedents and offered opinions on court matters.

EDUCATION

UNIVERSITY OF NEW YORK, SCHOOL OF LAW
Juris Doctor, May 1984
Class rank: Top Third
Dean's List (4 of 6 semesters)
Recipient, Andy Amos Award for Estates and Trusts
Recipient, American Law Student Award for Estates and Trusts
SemiFinalist Moot Court Competition

UNIVERSITY OF ARIZONA
Bachelor of Arts Degree in English
Recipient, Arizona Achievement Academic Scholarship
Pi Sigma Pi

MARY FERNANDEZ
21 LAFFER WAY
TAOS, NEW MEXICO 55667   907-555-7622

EMPLOYMENT BACKGROUND

1988 to Present   Jackson & Young
                                Associate

Focussed on the fields of Bankruptcy, Labor/Employment and Commercial
Litigation. Multi practice firm comprised of approximately 100 attorneys.

1985 to 1988   Tormay & Yuston
                                Associate

Coordinated with senior level partners who were involved in a variety of
areas of law including Environmental Law, Bankruptcy Law and Commercial
Transactions. Firms was comprised of approximately 230 attorneys.

1984-1985   The Honorable Manuel Notego
                                United States District Judge
                                Law Clerk

Assisted in researching precedents and opinions to support the Judge in
preparing key decisions. Reviewed precedents and offered opinions on court
matters.

EDUCATION

UNIVERSITY OF LOS ANGELES, SCHOOL OF LAW
Juris Doctor, May 1984
Class rank: Top Half
Dean's List
Recipient, Torgetto Award
Recipient, American Law Student Award for Ethics
Finalist Moot Court Competition

UNIVERSITY OF NEW MEXICO
Bachelor of Arts Degree in Spanish

References available upon request

MARY MCGRATH
12 OAK DR.
EDMONTON, KS 77654   (607)555-2345

EDUCATION   UNIVERSITY OF KANSAS
                     Candidate for Juris Doctor Degree
                     Honors: Executive Editorial Board and
Business Manager of the Bankruptcy Developments Journal;
Member of the Moot Court Society

                     UNIVERSITY OF PENNSYLVANIA
                     Bachelor of Arts, Major in English

                     CITY OF LONDON EXTENSION
                     Study Abroad, Interdisciplinary

PUBLICATIONS   BANKRUPTCY DEVELOPMENTS JOURNAL:Authored
article entitled "Recent Developments in Bankruptcy Law-
Appointments, Rights and Remedies of a Trustee."

ACTIVITIES   LAW SCHOOL-NITA Program Participant,
Student Legal Services, Tax Preparer for VITA Program,
Member of Sports and Entertainment Law Society, Student
Advisor to incoming law students.

LEGAL
EXPERIENCE   CARLTO COUNTY ATTORNEY"S OFFICE
                     Legal Internship: Active involvement in
all aspects of the prosecutor's office pursuant tot Kansas
Third Year Practice Act. Courtroom experience and
involvement in plea negotiations and drafting of
indictments and trial briefs.

                     JACKSON & BARNES
                     Summer Associate: Researched and wrote
legal briefs. Filed motion papers and memoranda in real
estate, labor, employment discrimination and negligence
cases. Assisted in closings, digested depositions and
attended pretrial conferences.

                     CHIEF JUDGE ALICE YOUNG UNITED STATES
BANKRUPTCY COURT
                     Judicial Clerkship: Researched and
drafted opinions on bankruptcy cases and proceedings.
Acted as Courtroom Deputy and observed adversary
proceedings, motion practices and Section 341 meetings.

NADINE SEPTEMBER
56 HOLLY STREET
JOHNSON, IL 61023
(312)555-5678

EDUCATION: BUTLER UNIVERSITY
                      SCHOOL OF LAW
                      Candidate for Juris Doctor Degree
                      National Association for Trial Advocacy
                      Registered for Illinois Bar Exam

                      UNIVERSITY OF ILLINOIS
                      B.A. History, Cum Laude
                      Grade Point Average: 3.78/4.0

ACTIVITIES &
HONORS: Phi Beta Kappa, Phi Kappa Phi, Golden Key
National Honor Society, Dean's List, Defender/Advocate Society, Criminal
Justice Society

LEGAL RELATED
EXPERIENCE: STATE OF ILLINOIS, DISTRICT ATTORNEY'S
                      OFFICE
                      Legal Intern: Involved in all aspects of prosecutor's
office including courtroom experience, drafting of indictments, and plea
negotiations.

                      ILLINOIS BAR ASSOCIATION
                      Worked closely with the Senior Director in
providing support services to the local legal community.

                      RAQUEL ROACH, DIRECTOR OF THE
                      COURT/CIVIL ARBITRATION
                      ADMINISTRATION
                      Assistant to the Court Administrator:
Responsibilities included developing and implementing new procedures,
scheduling arbitrators, and preparing statistical data.

                      POSTAL SERVICE SOLICITORS OFFICE
                      Intern: Assisted the Solicitors in interviewing
complainants, gathering evidence, and coordinating witnesses.

Continued on next page

NADINE SEPTEMBER   Page 2

THE HONORABLE STEVEN COD
Intern: Responsibilities included organizing activities of the Governmental Operations Committee and tracking legislation.

INTERESTS: Running, tennis, horticulture, and reading. Personally financed 100% of undergraduate and law school education.

NANCY CULPEPPER
45 THIRD AVE
UTICA, NY 44822   (607)555-2764

OBJECTIVE: A position in compensation, benefits or labor relations that would use my legal education and related experience.

EXPERIENCE:	BALCO MANUFACTURING	1983-Present
	Manager of Labor Relations	1988-Present
	Human Resources Ass't	1985-1988
	Staff Attorney	1984-1985
	LONGSDORF & ERLING	1982-1983
	Associate	

EDUCATION: UNIVERSITY OF NEW YORK, SCHOOL OF LAW
J.D. 1982

UNIVERSITY OF VERMONT
B.A., ENGLISH, 1979

HUMAN RESOURCES EXPERIENCE

Designed and implemented a pay-for-performance system and an innovative recognition & reward program.

Designed, negotiated, implemented, and administered employee benefit plans.

Implemented and administered 401(k) plans.

Administered salaried and hourly pension plans.

Managed compensation and benefits consolidations.

Trained supervisors on conducting effective performance appraisals.

Proactive participant in employee counseling and implementation of progressive discipline.

NANCY MAY   56 MAIN STREET   CHICAGO, IL 61023
(312)555-5678

EDUCATION: NORTHWESTERN UNIVERSITY
                    SCHOOL OF LAW 1994
                    Candidate for Juris Doctor Degree
                    National Institute for Trial Advocacy
                    Registered for Illinois Bar Exam

                    UNIVERSITY OF GEORGIA 1991
                    B.A. Criminal Justice, Cum Laude
                    Grade Point Average: 3.78/4.0

ACTIVITIES &
HONORS: Phi Beta Kappa, Phi Kappa Phi, Golden Key
National Honor Society, Dean's List, Defender/Advocate Society,
Criminal Justice Society.

LEGAL RELATED
EXPERIENCE: WAYMOUTH COUNTY DISTRICT
ATTORNEY'S OFFICE. 1993-94
                    Legal Intern: Involved in all aspects of
prosecutor's office including courtroom experience, drafting of
indictments and plea negotiations.

                    ILLINOIS BAR ASSOCIATION 1992-1993
                    Worked closely with the Executive Director in
providing support services to the local Bar membership.

                    ROCKBRIDGE COUNTY SUPERIOR
COURT/CIVIL ARBITRATION 1991-1992
                    Assistant to the Court Administrator:
Responsibilities included developing and implementing new
procedures, scheduling arbitrators, and preparing statistical data.

                    LOKLIN COUNTY SOLICITORS OFFICE
                    Intern: Assisted the Solicitors in interviewing
complainants, gathering evidence, and coordinating witnesses.

                    THE HONORABLE CULVER JONES
                    Intern: Responsibilities included organizing
activities of the Governmental Operations Committee and tracking
legislation.

INTERESTS: Running, tennis, horticulture, and reading.
Personally financed 100% of undergraduate and law school
education.

NANCY OSCARSTEIN
3 WILLOW LANE
ALBANY, AL 44576
(607)555-2764

EXPERIENCE: JACKSON FOODS: 1983-Present
                Manager of Employee & Labor Relations   1988-Present
                Human Resources Supervisor   1985-1988
                Staff Attorney   1984-1985

                HELD & BELLOW   1982-1983
                Associate

EDUCATION: UNIVERSITY OF BIRMINGHAM, SCHOOL OF LAW
                J.D. 1982

                UNIVERSITY OF ALABAMA
                B.A., ENGLISH, 1979

EXPERIENCE IN HUMAN RESOURCES

Proactive participant in employee counseling and implementation of progressive discipline.

Participated as a member of the management contract negotiating team.

Implemented and administered 401(k) plans.

Administered salaried and hourly pension plans.

Managed compensation and benefits consolidations.

Designed and implemented a pay-for-performance system and an innovative recognition & reward program.

Designed, negotiated, implemented, and administered employee benefit plans.

Trained supervisors on conducting effective performance appraisals.

PAUL PETERS
765 MOBERLY AVE
TULSA, OK 77687   (605)555-3276

BAR MEMBERSHIPS: OKLAHOMA & TEXAS

LEGAL EXPERIENCE: ASSOCIATE
                           BREMLIN, KEYS & DANFORTH
                           1987-PRESENT

                           LAW CLERK
                           HADWIN & SCHUSTER
                           SUMMER 1986

                           RESEARCH ASSISTANT
                           PROFS. QUINN, CONTRARO & YOUNG
                           UNIVERSITY OF OKLAHOMA
                           1985-1986

GOVERNMENT
EXPERIENCE: STAFF ASSISTANT
                           CONGRESSMAN PAUL GROVER
                           SUMMER 1984

                           RESEARCH ASSISTANT
                           CONSERVATIVE PARTY OF ENGLAND

EDUCATION: UNIVERSITY OF OKLAHOMA
                           J.D. 1989

                           LONDON LAW PROGRAM
                           1988

                           ST. MARY'S COLLEGE
                           B.A. HISTORY, 1986

MILITARY
EXPERIENCE: FIRST LIEUTENANT
                           UNITED STATES ARMY RESERVE

RAUMAN H. RAIJALH
7 MOLEBY AVE.
TULSA, OK 77687   (605)555-3276

BAR MEMBERSHIPS: OKLAHOMA & TEXAS

LEGAL EXPERIENCE: ASSOCIATE
                        ACWORTH & THOMAS
                        1989-PRESENT

                        LAW CLERK
                        FYNDE & LOSTEE
                        SUMMER 1988

                        RESEARCH ASSISTANT
                        PROFs. LOCKLAND & STRONG
                        UNIVERSITY OF OKLAHOMA
                        1985-1986

GOVERNMENT
EXPERIENCE: STAFF ASSISTANT
                        CONGRESSPERSON SARAH CENTER
                        SUMMER 1984

                        RESEARCH ASSISTANT
                        CONSERVATIVE PARTY OF GERMANY

EDUCATION: TULSA UNIVERSITY
                        J.D. 1989

                        MADRID LAW PROGRAM
                        1988

                        UNIVERSITY OF OKLAHOMA
                        B.A. HISTORY, 1986

MILITARY
EXPERIENCE: LT. COLONEL
                        UNITED STATES ARMY RESERVE

RACHEL BAKI
1286 BROOKSTONE DR
BELMONT, AR 44565
(908)555-8765

EDUCATION

Legal   Hope University, School of Law
                         Juris Doctor, cum laude, 1987
                              Class Standing: 25/175
                              GPA: 3.052

Undergraduate   Simmons College
                         Bachelor of Arts, cum laude, 1984
                              Phi Beta Kappa
                              GPA: 3.85

EMPLOYMENT
1989 to Present: Loser & Parselek, P.C.
                   Associate

Areas of concentration are insurance law, personal injury,
employment law, land use, and products liability.

Responsibilities include drafting appellate briefs and oral
arguments before the Arkansas and federal courts. Conduct
research and analysis of various substantive and
procedural issues.

Representative Reported Opinions:
                   Larson v Admar Foundation
                   Lung v Trotter
                   Boise Gas v Allentown
                   Kismo v Garble
                   Unread v Boston

1987 to 1989   Arkansas Court of Appeals
                   Law Clerk to the Hon. Bruce Cabot

RITA JONES
45 LONG BOAT WAY
MIAMI, FLORIDA 45667
(709)555-8833

EDUCATION   UNIVERSITY OF MIAMI
                             SHULA SCHOOL OF LAW
                             J.D. 1985
                                     Honors: Finalist, Moot Court
                             Competition, 1984 &1985

                             FLORIDA STATE UNIVERSITY
                             B.A., Philosophy, 1982

EXPERIENCE   DEIRDORFF & FRUMP
                             ASSOCIATE 1986-Present

Reduce large depositions to digest form and prepare litigation binders. Attend
trials and provide assistance to lead counsel. Serve as a senior associate for a
mid-sized defense firm specializing in medical malpractice litigation.
Conducted legal and medical research and draft memoranda. Analyze prior
testimony of medical experts called to testify against our clients.

                             HONORABLE B. CRABB
                             DISTRICT COURT OF FLORIDA
                             LAW CLERK 1985-1986

Researched the insurability of Rule 21 sanctions, the admissibility of victim
impact statements, and the validity of family exclusion clauses in airline
insurance contracts. Prepared memoranda on issues in pending cases.

                             HONORABLE JACK GLEASON
                             UNITED STATES DISTRICT JUDGE
                             LAW INTERN Summer 1984

Areas researched included habeas corpus and the use of the Waste Treatment
Act of 1980 as a defense to anti-dumping provisions. Attended pretrial
conferences, jury selections, hearings, and trials. Researched law and helped
draft memoranda, orders, and opinions.

ROB HALO
23 ACCESS BLVD.
HOUSTON, TX 44587   (504)555-7623

HOUSTON BANCORP   1980-Present
ASSOCIATE CORPORATE COUNSEL

Responsible for the legal functions relating to corporate practice, governance, and insurance. Particular emphasis on anti-takeover, 16b, and Corporate Code of Conduct issues. Designed and executed revisions of the director/officer liability and indemnification policy.

Organized and executed a compliance review of all company owned real estate with sale and lease-back requirements, including title insurance and surveys.

Designed and wrote three non-qualified management incentive plans with related deferred funds and three non-qualified performance unit plans. Sole in-house counsel on numerous pension, stock option, 401(K), ESOP, Supplemental Executive, and welfare benefit plans.

Extensive experience in negotiation of performance plan design and administration, drafting and substantive review of outside counsels drafts for consistency and accuracy.

Monitored and directed litigation involving potential contingent liability of $100m.

Developed, executed and maintained all legal documentation pertaining to the CIRRUS electronic banking network.

Negotiated and wrote financing, banking, and fund transfer agreements for the Treasurer's office as well as term and revolving credit agreements, letters of credit documentation, loan participations, guaranties, equipment lease pricing, state of the art equipment purchase contracts for Corporate Banking, Corporate Finance, International and Corporate Services.

Responsible for regulatory analysis on financial services issues including investment services, electronic banking, and securities product development.

Negotiated and wrote computer equipment contracts, software licenses, and computer service agreement for the company.

EDUCATION

UNIVERSITY OF HOUSTON
J.D. 1980
Editor of Banking & Legal Issues Review

UNIVERSITY OF TEXAS
B.A. SOCIOLOGY 1977

Admitted to the Texas and Oklahoma Bar

STANLEY BING
22 LONG ROAD
PHILADELPHIA, PA 77445   (608)555-8833

ARMOUNT REFINING & PROCESSING   1981 to Present
Vice President Legal

Reduced substantial backlog of litigation and successfully managed affairs of the company to avoid significant new lawsuits despite challenging and changing business environments.

Employed innovative approaches to obtain directors' and officers' liability insurance during turbulent times for the company.

Restructured controllership function thereby increasing productivity in the consolidation area by 30%.

ALLIED INDUSTRIES   1977-1981
Vice President of Taxes

Responsible for minimizing worldwide tax liability and exploiting tax planning opportunities. Key responsibilities included excess foreign tax credit utilization; expatriate tax planning; inter-company pricing; international treaty provisions; legal entity capitalization alternatives; short and long-term incentive arrangements; technology agreements; as well as federal, state, local, and foreign tax compliance.

Handled domestic and international tax research and planning covering audit negotiations, depreciation, and foreign tax credits. This included inventory absorption, redemption, reorganizations, and ruling requests.

Authorized development, evaluated, and approved implementation of inventory cycle counting procedures, eliminating need for annual physical inventory.

Decreased outside audit fees 23% by more effectively coordinating internal and external audits, implementing a plant self audit program, and revising audit scope coverage.

Continued

STANLEY BING   Page 2

Created the company's Internal Specialist Program. High potential individuals were given responsibility over specific legal areas. Specialists gained international experience and established key legal policies. Current staff was able to meet expanded needs.

Member of the Legal and Tax Institute of the American Bar Association.

Developed the Intensive Executive Development Workshop which was adopted by the firm worldwide.

EDUCATION

J.D. UNIVERSITY OF PENNSYLVANIA, 1977

M.S. FINANCE, UNIVERSITY OF PENNSYLVANIA, 1974

M.B.A. (Concentration in Finance), HAMPTON COLLEGE, 1973

B.A., ECONOMICS, HAMPTON COLLEGE, 1971

ADDITIONAL TRAINING

YALE UNIVERSITY, FINANCIAL MANAGEMENT PROGRAM

WHARTON BUSINESS SCHOOL, MANAGERIAL NEGOTIATIONS

SUSAN ST. MARIE
23 Dribble Ave.
Allentown, PA 56778   (807)555-9476

EDUCATION	University of Pennsylvania	
	J.D., 1989	

Connecticut College
B.A. 1986
Majors: Psychology & Dance

EXPERIENCE

Associate   1989 to Present
BOYD, BASKIN & SELLS

Assist senior partners serving clients in the high technology industries. Prepare briefs, research precedents, and interact with members of the client's legal staff.

Serve as mentor to newly recruited staff members and play an active role in the firm's recruitment activities on the University of Pennsylvania campus.

Law Clerk
HAYDEN CABLE ASSOCIATES

Interpreted and evaluated cable television franchise agreements. Researched key issues and drafted appropriate documents.

Assisted Counsel with general corporate legal duties.

Mortgage Clerk
MBN CREDIT SERVICES

Acquired insight into the home loan application process.

Gained experience communicating by phone with clients.

Administrative Assistant
GOLMAN CAPITAL MANAGEMENT

Handled financial aspects of a small investment advisory firm in addition to performing secretarial and administrative duties.

House-fellow
CONNECTICUT COLLEGE

TAMI ROGERS
12 TATE RD
LINCOLN, MA. 09887
(617)555-9866

EDUCATION   **UNIVERSITY OF BOSTON**
                       J.D. DEGREE, 1989
                       GPA 85.31
                       RANK 24/131
                       ACTIVITIES AND HONORS
                             LAWS REVIEW
                             NOTE AND COMMENT EDITOR
                             DEAN'S LIST

                       UNIVERSITY OF MASSACHUSETTS
                       B.A. SOCIOLOGY, 1986
                       ACTIVITIES AND HONORS
                             DEAN'S LIST
                             SENATOR-STUDENT ASSOCIATION
                             VP-RESIDENTIAL GROUP COUNCIL

PUBLICATIONS   "The Corporate Opportunity Doctrine:
An Examination of Precedents and Opportunities."
American Journal of Contract Law, September 1991

PROFESSIONAL EXPERIENCE

LACY & LACY   1990 to Present
ASSOCIATE

THE HONORABLE JACKSON LANT
MASSACHUSETTS COURT OF APPEALS, EASTERN DISTRICT
LAW CLERK   1989-1990

BROWN, JONES & GIVENS
LAW CLERK   1987-1988

JAMIL BRAMEUL
12 TOLL ROAD
CLEVELAND OHIO 55943   (807)555-7865

OHIO STATE UNIVERSITY
J.D., 1980

MIAMI UNIVERSITY OF OHIO
B.A., HISTORY 1977

PROFESSIONAL EXPERIENCE:

ARMONK FOODS   1980-Present
Vice President/Associate General Counsel   1988-Present

Directed management in development of sales and product strategies
resulting in increases in sales from $1 million to $7 million annually.
Additionally, coordinated the private placement of over $5 million in
preferred stock.

Developed and negotiated contracts for nationwide introduction of Vovoom
Cheese Spread and successfully addressed concerns of the Food and Drug
Administration.

Represented the company on boards of directors of two company owned
subsidiaries.

Directed the Law Department response to broad scope of sales and marketing
efforts in contractual and product development areas. These included major
customer and vendor relationships and new product strategies.

Developed contracts and participated in design of product introduction
strategy for nationwide introduction of Nature's Choice Pizza Kits.

DIRECTOR, LEGAL & ADMINISTRATIVE SERVICES   1980-1988

Negotiated innovative office space lease that resulted in $800,000 cash income
prior to occupancy.

Continued on next page

Managed and directed the activities of 3 attorneys and 15 support personnel.

Managed all corporate and regulatory legal functions. As head of Administrative Services managed all facilities and internal services including purchasing, word processing, and facilities management.

Negotiated 21 creative lease and construction agreements to establish four food manufacturing plants in the midwest.

```
THELMA DELBELLO
87 RIDGE RD.
CARLSON, CA  98443
(304)555-8963
```

AREAS OF LEGAL EXPERTISE:

MARKETING AND PUBLIC RELATIONS:

Presented numerous seminars to lenders, title insurers, and attorneys on the legal aspects of originating mortgages which conform to the secondary mortgage market.

Originated and participated in our company's legal/marketing team and obtained an increased market share in North Carolina through aggressive proactive business development and customer service efforts.

NEGOTIATIONS AND LEGAL REPRESENTATION:

Negotiated changes for approval of legal documentation in two developments, which created large unique retirement/recreational communities in California, making $50 million in investments available to our company.

Negotiated changes in complex legal documentation, on-site, at a cooperative housing development in Los Angeles, making available $2 million in new investments.

EMPLOYMENT EXPERIENCE

FEDERAL NATIONAL MORTGAGE ASSOCIATION   1983-PRESENT
Senior Counsel

EDUCATION

UCLA, SCHOOL OF LAW, 1983, J.D.
Editorial Staff, Journal of Public Law

UCLA, A.B. Liberal Arts, Major History, 1980
Additionally, completed partial credits for MBA in Finance and International Business at UCLA.

THOMAS QUICKSILVER JR.
12 HEDGE DRIVE
JOHNSON CITY, TN 33455   **(807)555-7865**

BACKGROUND SUMMARY: Highly experienced executive with both legal and line responsibilities. Particular expertise in start-up and development stage enterprises.

PROFESSIONAL EXPERIENCE:

US TELECOM   **1980-Present**
Vice President/Associate General Counsel   **1988-Present**

Led Law Department response to broad scope of sales and marketing efforts in contractual and product development areas. These included major customer and vendor relationships and new product strategies.

Developed contracts and participated in design of product introduction strategy for nationwide introduction of Nation-Phone service.

Developed and negotiated contracts for nationwide introduction of SAFEBLOCK service and service offerings for the state government market.

Represented the company on boards of directors of two start-up ventures.

Assisted management in development of sales and product strategies resulting in increases in sales from $1 million to $7 million annually. Additionally, coordinated the private placement of over $5 million in preferred stock.

DIRECTOR, LEGAL & ADMINISTRATIVE SERVICES 1980-1988

Managed all corporate and regulatory legal function for this start-up long distance communications company. As head of Administrative Services managed all facilities and internal services including purchasing, word processing, and facilities management.

Negotiated 21 creative lease and construction agreements to establish a nationwide satellite communications network.

Negotiated innovative office space lease that resulted in $800,000 cash income prior to occupancy.

Negotiated flexible $1 million volume purchase agreement for satellite earth stations.

Managed and directed the activities of 3 attorneys and 15 support personnel.

EDUCATION

VANDERBILT UNIVERSITY
JD, 1980

COLGATE UNIVERSITY
BA, HISTORY 1977

TIM RASTA
1208 LASTER LANE
DALLAS, TEXAS 675332   (503)555-2398

UNIVERSITY OF TEXAS, SCHOOL OF LAW
Candidate for combined Juris Doctor and Master's in Business
Administration degrees.

HONORS: Selected for inclusion in the 23rd edition of Who's Who Among
American Law Students. Member of the Editorial Board, Business Manager
and a Recent Developments Editor: Bankruptcy Developments Journal.

ACTIVITIES: Member, Association for Business Professionalism; Member,
JD/MBA Society; Member, Student Bar Association; Member, Legal
Association of Law Students; Head Judge, Intercollegiate Business Games
Organization.

TEXAS A&M, SCHOOL OF BUSINESS
Bachelor of Science in Business Administration 1981
Majors: Finance and Economics; GPA 3.72/4.0

HONORS: Dean's List for all semesters, Academic Scholarship, International
Economic Honor Society, Texas A&M Board of Trustees.

ACTIVITIES: President, University of Texas Students in Free Enterprise; Vice-
President of Finance, The Society for the Advancement of Management.

PUBLICATIONS: Author, Legal Response to Three Mile Fishing Limitations.

EXPERIENCE

SUMMER ASSOCIATE
Texas Southern Bank
Assisted several branch banks in preparing for an important audit by the
United States Banking Service.Wrote Texas Southern's annual Proxy
Statement and Form 10-K in compliance with federal securities laws. Wrote
the bank's new employee stock option plan. Assisted outside counsel in
meeting Internal Revenue Code requirements for qualifying the bank's
amended retirement plan. 1992

Continued

TIM RASTA   Page 2

TRADER   1981-1992
Goldman Brothers
Answered client inquiries about financial implications of investment
operations. Advised clients of their rights and alternatives in a merger or
tender offer. Supervised stock transfer for the brokerage clients of over 20
affiliated banks. Specialized in the legal requirements and ramifications of
trading restricted stock. Rule 144 stock and stock for estates, trusts,
corporations, and partnerships.

References available upon request

TOM BRINKMAN
8 LARSON RD.
BUFFALO GROVE, IL 60087
(708)555-7344

LEGAL EXPERTISE:

BUSINESS DEVELOPMENT

Author of numerous articles read by lenders, title insurers, and attorneys on the legal aspects of originating mortgages which conform to the secondary mortgage market.

Serve in a leadership role for the company's legal/marketing team. Efforts of the team resulted in increased market share in Illinois largely as a result of aggressive proactive business development and customer service efforts.

NEGOTIATING SKILLS

Successfully negotiated contract changes for two developments, which resulted in the creation of the largest mixed-use residential/business community in Illinois. Negotiated with the investment banking community a $50 million investment currently available to our company.

Negotiated changes in legal documentation for a cooperative housing development in Chicago, thus making available over $12 million in new investments.

EMPLOYMENT EXPERIENCE

JACKSON & JOHNSON MORTGAGE BROKERS   1983–Present
Vice President Legal Affairs
Chief Counsel
Staff Attorney

EDUCATION

University of Chicago, 1983, J.D.
Editorial Staff, Journal of Corporate Law

DePaul University, A.B. Liberal Arts, Major History, 1980
Additionally, completed partial credits for M.B.A. in Finance and International Business at Northwestern University.

References available upon request

TONY EVANGELLI
1208 CAROL LANE
DAYTON, OH 67532   (503)555-2398

UNIVERSITY OF DAYTON, SCHOOL OF LAW
Candidate for combined Juris Doctor and Masters in Business Administration degrees.

HONORS: Member of the Editorial Board, Business Manager, and a Recent Developments Editor: Bankruptcy Developments Journal. Selected for inclusion in the 4th edition of Who's Who Among American Law Students.

ACTIVITIES: Member JD/MBA Society; Member, Student Bar Association; Member, Legal Association of Law Students; Head Judge, Intercollegiate Business Games Organization; Member, Association for Business Professionalism.

UNIVERSITY OF DAYTON, SCHOOL OF COMMERCE
Bachelor of Science in Business Administration 1981
Majors: Finance and Economics; GPA 3.72/4.0

HONORS: Order Sons of Italy in America Academic Scholarship, International Economic Honor Society, University of Dayton Board of Trustees, Dean's List for all semesters.

ACTIVITIES: President, University of Dayton Students in Free Enterprise; Vice-President of Finance, The Society for the Advancement of Management.

PUBLICATIONS: Author, The Reorganization Process: Bankruptcy Developments Journal.

EXPERIENCE

SUMMER ASSOCIATE-CORPORATE SECRETARY'S OFFICE
Jackson Industries
Wrote Jackson's annual Proxy Statement and Form 10-K in compliance with federal securities laws. Wrote Jackson's new employee stock option plan. Assisted outside counsel in meeting Internal Revenue Code requirements for qualifying Jackson's amended retirement plan. Assisted one of Jackson's New York Divisions in preparing for an important audit by the United States Customs Service.

RESEARCH ASSISTANT
University of Dayton School of Law
Assisted two professors in researching and preparing a paper on the legal and economic implications of a National Market System.

WAYNE SUSSMAN
24 TOAD POND ROAD
UTICA, NEW YORK 45009
(897)555-5894

EDUCATION   UNIVERSITY OF NEW YORK-UTICA
Candidate for Juris Doctor Degree
Class rank: 24/106

UNIVERSITY OF UTICA
B.A. Economics
GPA: 3.7/4.0

HONORS &
ACTIVITIES   LAW SCHOOL: Dean's Advisory Committee,
Managing Editor Utica Law Journal, Dean's List, Three-quarter tuition merit
scholarship.

UNDERGRADUATE: University Task Force on
Greek Housing, Student Alumni association, Campus judicial Board, Honors
College, William Randolph Hearst Foundation Scholarship Recipient,
Gamma Beta Phi Honor Society, Alpha Lamda Delta Honor Society.

EXPERIENCE   MARPAN, KRAVEN & STACEY, Summer
Associate
Worked exclusively in the real estate practice area.
Drafted briefs and legal memoranda.

RANDALL & CONNORS, Summer Associate
Worked in the trust and real estate practice areas.
Conducted legal research and drafted a variety of briefs and legal memoranda.

KENT, JAMESON & THORN, Summer Associate
Worked in the litigation, corporate, and real estate
practice areas. Prepared legal memoranda and loan agreement modifications.
Reviewed proposed contract provisions between lenders and clients.

WENDY SHOENFELDT
2345 CARLSON WAY
DALLAS, TX 55677
(897)555-5894

EDUCATION   **UNIVERSITY OF DALLAS**
Candidate for Juris Doctor Degree
Class rank: 23/106

UNIVERSITY OF TEXAS
B.A. Economics
GPA: 3.7/4.0, 1991

HONORS &
ACTIVITIES   LAW SCHOOL: Managing Editor Dallas Law Journal,
Deans List, Three-quarter tuition merit scholarship, Dean's Advisory Committee.

UNDERGRADUATE: UT Honors College, William
Randolph Hearst Foundation Scholarship Recipient, Gamma Beta Phi Honor
Society, Alpha Lambda Delta Honor Society, University Task Force on Greek
Housing, Student Alumni Association, Campus Judicial Board.

EXPERIENCE   **LASKIN, JONES & MAZE**, Summer Associate
Worked exclusively in the litigation practice area.
Drafted briefs and legal memoranda.

ALSON & CROW, Summer Associate
Worked in the litigation and corporate practice areas.
Conducted legal research and drafted a variety of briefs and legal memoranda.

CATHCHY & DOBBS, Summer Associate
Worked in the litigation, corporate, and real estate
practice areas. Prepared legal memoranda and loan agreement modifications.
Reviewed proposed contract provisions between lenders and clients.

NELSON & QUICK, Summer Associate
Worked primarily in the firm's litigation area.

References available upon request

WESTIN CARTWRIGHT III
12 LOVE DRIVE
OCEAN BREEZE, CT 06457   754-555-0987

YALE UNIVERSITY
SCHOOL OF LAW, Candidate for Juris Doctor Degree

Honors: Moot Court Semifinalist

Activities: Moot Court Participant, Volunteer for Student Legal Services, member International Law Society.

Internship: Department of Health and Human Services
Responsibilities include researching topics on health, exclusion, and rescission of adjustment status. Authored memoranda regarding programs involving developmental needs and immediate relative status. Prepared briefs submitted to the Board of Appeals. Attended court held before the Subcommittee on Aging.

UNIVERSITY OF CHICAGO
Bachelor of Arts Degree in History and Political Science
Honors: Selected for law internship. Dean's List.
Activities: Student Pre-Law Committee. Political Science and History Academies.

UPTONVILLE INTERNATIONAL UNIVERSITY
Intensive summer Greek Language Program. Activities included seminars in Cyprus and other travel.

LEGAL EMPLOYMENT

RESEARCH ASSISTANT, Yale University School of Law

Researched and wrote memoranda concerning the state of requirements for constitutional torts and the reopening of administrative hearings in social security, selective service, and immigration cases. Extensive use of law library, LEXIS, and Westlaw systems. Enhanced research and writing skills.

Continued

WESTIN CARTWRIGHT III   Page 2

PARALEGAL, Mark Canton, Counsellor at Law

Followed trade legislation, anti-dumping, and countervailing cases. Gained insight into the workings of international trade, government agencies, and congressional offices. Assisted with preparation of briefs submitted to federal agencies. Researched areas of barter, countertrade, and Generalized System of Preferences.

LAW CLERK, Karen Summers Esq.

Assisted with research regarding tax sales, trusts, personal injuries, and landlord-tenant disputes. Prepared residential lease agreements, attended client interviews, and served process. Gained exposure to small private practice.

References available upon request

WILMA RUBBLE
123 TORUK AVE.
BARNSTABLE, MA 98776   617-555-0987

HARVARD UNIVERSITY
SCHOOL OF LAW, Candidate for Juris Doctor Degree

Honors: Moot Court Semifinalist

Activities: Moot Court Participant, Volunteer for Student Legal Services, member
International Law Society.

Internship: Department of Justice, Immigration and Naturalization Service
Responsibilities include researching topics on deportation, exclusion, and rescission of
adjustment status. Authored memoranda regarding crimes involving moral turpitude and
visa requests for immediate relative status. Prepared briefs submitted to the Board of
Immigration Appeals. Attended court held before the Immigration Judge.

TUFTS UNIVERSITY
Bachelor of Arts Degree in History and Political Science
Honors: Selected for Washington, DC law internship. Dean's List.
Activities: Student Pre-Law Committee. Political Science and History Academies.

SCHILLER INTERNATIONAL UNIVERSITY
Intensive summer German Language Program. Activities included seminars in East and
West Berlin and other travel.

LEGAL EMPLOYMENT

RESEARCH ASSISTANT, Harvard University School of Law

Researched and wrote memoranda concerning the state of requirements for constitutional
torts and the reopening of administrative hearings in social security, selective service, and
immigration cases. Extensive use of law library, LEXIS and Westlaw systems. Enhanced
research and writing skills.

PARALEGAL, Robert S. Balik, Counsellor at Law

Assisted with preparation of briefs submitted to federal agencies. Researched areas of
barter, countertrade, and Generalized System of Preferences. Followed trade legislation,
anti-dumping, and countervailing cases. Gained insight into the workings of international
trade, government agencies, and congressional offices.

LAW CLERK, Martin Wolczyk Esq.

Assisted with research regarding tax sales, trusts, personal injuries, and landlord-tenant
disputes. Prepared residential lease agreements, attended client interviews, and served
process. Gained exposure to small private practice.

DOT SAMUELS
123 OCEAN SIDE DRIVE
TETTLEY, TN 22334
(608)885-9833

SUMMARY: Highly competent researcher and expert in tax, and other financial compliance areas. Energetic and enthusiastic. Highly experienced at working with a diverse group of clients and judges. Able to relate effectively and efficiently to colleagues and senior level managers.

EXPERIENCE: TENNESSEE MOGUL   1979 to Present

1989-Present: Senior Staff Attorney

        Responsible for the efficient legal representation of over 350 cases. Assisted in the conversion of the legal administration system process form a manual approach to a computerized system. Increased levels of customer satisfaction based on annual client surveys of the legal process.

        Organized and implemented an annual symposium on legal issues facing our industry. Attracted over 123 attorneys representing industry groups, corporations, and law firms. Received positive feedback on the event from senior management as an effective tool for increasing awareness of the company among a variety of constituents.

1979-1989:   Staff Attorney

        Provided legal support to the Vice President of Legal Affairs for the corporation. Coordinated support staff and conducted research on all tax, compliance, and regulatory issues. Handled daily court appearances and routine legal matters. Served as the company facilitator for industry round tables.

Continued

DOT SAMUELS   Page 2

EDUCATION: University of Mechlenberg
                  J.D., Cum Laude, 1979
                  Assistant Editor, Mechlenberg Law Review

                  University of Tennessee
                  B.A. Philosophy, 1976

Reference provided upon request

CARL CHANG
1 MEADOW LANE
ARLINGTON, VA 55465
(809)555-4433

OBJECTIVE: A position utilizing my background in military law and over thirty years of service in the United States Army. Plan to retire from active duty this year, with the rank of Major.

SUMMARY: Extensive experience in research, litigation, and negotiations. Ability to relate effectively to enlisted personnel, senior-level officers, and high-ranking civilian personnel. Adept at the management of the military legal system and its interactions with the civilian bar.

EDUCATION:
GEORGE MASON UNIVERSITY
J.D., 1965

ARMY INTELLIGENCE INSTITUTE
M.A. MILITARY SCIENCE, 1962

THE CITADEL
B.A., ENGLISH, 1961

EXPERIENCE:
UNITED STATES ARMY   1965 to Present
Chief Legal Officer   1984 to Present

Coordinate all legal activities for the 195th Joint Infantry. In addition to day-to-day legal operations, am responsible for the dissemination of information from various Senate and House committees to senior command officers in the joint forces. Coordinate preparation of all ongoing litigation and plea bargaining. Supervise a staff of 27.

Senior Attorney   1976-1984

Provided tactical and technical legal information and feedback to the Commanding Officer 7th Battalion, Korea. Personally conducted all significant trial work. Managed a staff of 15.

Attorney   1971-1976

Served in he number two legal position to the chief attorney of Ft. Johnston. Supervised a staff of 21 attorneys and paralegals. Responsible for all day-to-day legal activity. Awarded Army citation for excellence.

ERIC VON LUSTBATER
123 MAIN STREET
DAYTON, OH   30021
513-765-4433

OBJECTIVE: A position that would utilize my legal background in the HVAC industry.

EXPERIENCE: JOHNSTON CONTROLS, 1980 to Present

Responsible for all law department activities for this $76 million manufacturer of heating and air conditioning equipment.

Reduced liens against the corporation from $4 million to $123,000 during my tenure.

Initiated the recruitment of experienced staff attorneys which resulted in a reduction of overall legal costs by 23%.

Developed the Chinese Wall Defense, which resulted in a positive result for the corporation in 16 of 17 recent trials.

JACKSON & JACKSON, 1970-1980
Partner

Responsible for client development and law firm activity in the recreation and hospitality industries.

Increased trial wins by 67% through the introduction of innovative plaintiff defense arguments. Led the initiation and development of the firm's practice in this field.

Education: Hardwich University, Colleges of
                  Business & Law
                  B.S. Business and J.D.,1970

ARNOLD SMATZ
123 TRUCE ROAD
LOS ANGELES, CA 98744
(301)555-7766

EXECUTIVE SUMMARY: Proven ability to manage complex legal issues in normal and crisis situations. Able to create and implement legal strategies to improve firm market share and earnings. Record of stabilizing uncertainties during mergers, acquisitions, turnarounds, and restructurings. Leader and strong individual producer in relationships with clients, community groups, and regulators.

EXPERIENCE & ACCOMPLISHMENTS

BAXISS CORPORATION 1985 to Present
Vice President, Legal

Directed a staff of twenty responsible for improving the level of legal support for management objectives.

Anticipated business opposition to construction projects and plans for local commercial growth. Pro-actively responded to all issues and demonstrated the merits of alternative perspectives.

KURTIS, STRANE & HOPKINS 1977-1985
PARTNER   1981-1985
ASSOCIATE   1977-1981

Developed active and positive relations with security analysts, developers and other clients.

EDUCATION: J.D. University of California, 1977
                 B.A. Purdue University, 1974

References available upon request

ALLISON GOMEZ
LATNER PLACE
ATLANTA, GA   30098
(404)555-8866

LAUNDERS & PILSON   1971 to Present
Stone Mountain, GA

MANAGING PARTNER
Began as an associate with responsibility for clients in the textile and retail industries. Responsibilities grew to encompass management of large client relationships. Supervised the company's training and recruiting programs.

Promoted to Managing Partner in 1982 with added responsibility for the firm's marketing. Major accomplishments in this position included the following:

Increased local market share to 35% despite a severe overall reduction in the use of legal services by prime corporate clients.

Reestablished the firm's competitive position in the growing chemical market by recruiting partners with specific areas of expertise.

Maintained overall firm expense level at under 6% of revenues through such major innovation as establishing an in-house accounting and personnel functions.

Vastly improved the firm's image with local businesses through aggressive PR campaign coupled with outreach efforts by senior partners.

Acted as client's spokesperson on such delicate issues as gun control and product recalls.

EDUCATION: University of Georgia
                    B.A. English 1968, J.D. 1971

ALAN JARKOWITZ
4 CROW ST.
TRAMMEL, TX 55432
(303)555-9875

OBJECTIVE: A position in real estate law

EXPERIENCE:
BLUE BIRD DEVELOPMENT   1987-Present
Vice President Legal

Supervise 7 full-time and 5 part-time lawyers for this leading developer of apartment complexes and shopping centers.

Responsible for tax, compliance, and litigation services. Report to the CEO and Chairman.

Reduced quarterly and year end closings from 4 weeks to 10 days through the introduction of computerized legal software.

Achieved 100% accuracy in closing over 45 legal transactions each quarter.

Reduced processing time of legal claims from 4 months to 30 days.

FENWICK & FENWICK   1980-1987
Senior Associate

Conducted legal assignments in the real estate and oil and gas industries.

Received superior evaluations for applying innovative legal methods in solving client problems.

EDUCATION:

Southern Texas A&M, J.D., 1980
West Falls College B.A., 1977

ALI EL ABDULA
4 WALNUT ST.
LOS ANGELES, CA 97655
310-555-8874

OBJECTIVE: A position in the legal community which involves planning and coordination between support groups and clients.

STRENGTHS & SKILLS

PLANNING: Successfully directed the legal efforts for a wide range of companies and industries. Managed an in-house committee to provide real world perspective to local area law schools. Designed an interactive instruction program for law students. instructed on tax laws and compliance at several law schools.

MARKETING: Designed a successful marketing plan to attract new clients. Coordinated the media's coverage of our high profile position in Wade vs. Jackson. Wrote several speeches for senior partners. Assisted in the development of firm marketing materials.

COMMUNICATION: Conducted over 25 public presentations to local businesses and legal associations. Author of several articles promoting increased law firm involvement in civic activities. Significant experience as an adjunct instructor.

EDUCATION: J.D., University of California, 1976

B.A., Stanford University, 1973
Major, English

References furnished upon request.

ARNIE BURNS
21 WILSON ST.
ALLENTOWN, PA 33432
(907)555-9955

OBJECTIVE: A position utilizing my background and experience i legal issues impacting the financial and real estate industries.

EXPERIENCE: UNITED HOME MORTGAGE COMPANY, 1977-Present
                  CHIEF LEGAL OFFICER

Identified new areas for savings in legal feeds and assisted in the development of the company's first comprehensive marketing plan.

Negotiated a credit buy-back agreement with First National Corporation resulting in increased efficiencies in both companies' operations.

Developed a system to monitor legal trends in mortgage financing.

Negotiated a loan assumption which was three percentage points below the national average.

Coordinated the physical move of personnel and office equipment from St. Louis. Negotiated a new lease arrangement for the new office.

Liquidated excess inventory in conjunction with the move from St. Louis.

Drafted a feasibility study to determine the economic impact on the firm by an increase in mortgage rates.

EDUCATION: Washington University, 1977
                 B.A. Economics & J.D. with Honors

References available upon request

ALICE EL SANTIAGO
23 MILL WAY
MILWAUKEE, WI 87445
(907)555-6433

BARTON BREWING COMPANIES   1991-Present
STAFF ATTORNEY

Organized annual negotiation agreements for labor contracts which totalled $125 million annually and resulted in a $5 million annual savings against budget.

Coordinated centralized material distribution to ten breweries.

Restructured $10 million in corporate lease agreements for high speed packaging equipment.

Supervised two lawyers and recruited four additional interns from local area law schools.

Managed a variety of corporate programs totalling $60 million annually.

Negotiated Sparrow Snacks loan requirement, annual co-packer contracts, and premiums. Personally achieved annual savings of $200,000.

CLEANEASE CORPORATION   1980-1991
CHIEF COUNSEL

Responsible for all legal activities including regulatory compliance and contracts.

JOHNSTON & STEEL   1974-1980
STAFF ATTORNEY

Served clients in the real estate and petroleum industries.

MILITARY: Corporal, United States Army-Signal Corp., 1969-1971

EDUCATION: Whitewater University
            J.D., 1974

            Lyons University
            B.A., Political Science, 1969

References available upon request

ART HORDEN
123 WEST LANE
WILDWOOD, CO 65443
(513)555-8755

SUMMARY: Extensive experience in legal matters as they pertain to the retail and entertainment industries.

EXPERIENCE:

1980 to Present   ASTER & JONES
                                     PARTNER

Manage client relationships in key industries. Responsible for $2,000,000 in personal billing,

Serve as a mentor and coach to associates and junior partners.

Adapted a manual inventory control system with a computerized system through self study of Lotus 1-2-3.

Created an employee manual which was instrumental in increasing productivity and moral.

Improved collections by developing a seven step collection process and training personnel on its implementation.

1977 to 1980   OXMORE, GLAVIN, MASIUS & BERNIUS
                                     ASSOCIATE

Supported senior partners in the tax, compliance, and litigation areas. Developed clients in the entertainment and high technology fields.

EDUCATION: GREENBRIER UNIVERSITY
                                    J.D., 1977
                                    LAW REVIEW, HONORS GRADUATE

JEREMY   MENDEZ
65   THIRD   ST.
GROVE,   CA.   67443
(410)555-9247

EDUCATION:

UNIVERSITY   OF   CALIFORNIA   AT   LOS   ANGELES
COLLEGE   OF   LAW
J.D.   May   1987
Editor-in-Chief   UCLA   Law   Journal

HUMSTEAD   UNIVERSITY
B.A.   Philosophy,   1984
Magna   Cum   Laude
Research   Assistant,   Department   of   Philosophy
Commander,   Navel   Reserve   Officers   Training   Corps   Detachment
Agnes   Scott   Scholar
Who's   Who   Among   American   Scholars,   Varsity   Baseball,   ROTC,
Student   Government

PROFESSIONAL   EXPERIENCE:

SENIOR   ATTORNEY,   UNITED   STATES   NAVY
NAVY   THIRD   COMMAND   HEADQUARTERS
1991   to   Present

Provide   administrative   law   advice   and   opinions   and   administer   the
Navy's   internal   investigative   branch.

Devise   litigation   and   discovery   strategies   on   all   matters   pertaining
to   the   third   fleet   and   its   headquarter   support   staff.

Serve   as   lead   counsel   in   a   variety   of   cases   involving   Navy   interests
overseas.   Coordinate   legal   activities   between   the   Navy,   the
Pentagon,   and   the   National   Security   Agency   (NSA).

Manage   and   monitor   case-load   of   primary   federal   tort   and   criminal
litigation   involving   the   Navy.

Continued   on   next   page.

JEREMY MENDEZ   **Page 2**

**ATTORNEY, LITIGATION BRANCH, OFFICE OF THE NAVY STAFF
JUDGE ADVOCATE**
Headquarters, 4TH Fleet   1987-1991

Investigated, settled or recommended denial for federal tort claims filed against the U.S. Army totalling over $312 million.

In charge of adjudicating over 23 federal claims per year involving over $3 million.

ROBIN HUGHES
10 OXNARD RD
SAN DIEGO, CA 55684   (504)555-7623

SAN DIEGO TRUST CO.   1980-Present
CORPORATE ATTORNEY

Considerable experience in negotiation of performance plan design, and administration, drafting and substantive review of outside counsels drafts for consistency and accuracy.

Successfully negotiated and wrote computer equipment contracts, software licenses, and computer service agreement for the company.

Oversaw and personally directed litigation involving potential contingent liability of $45 million.

Designed and maintained all legal documentation pertaining to the CIRRUS electronic banking network.

Successfully negotiated and authored financing, banking, and fund transfer agreements for the Controller's office as well as term and revolving credit agreements, letters of credit documentation, loan participations, guaranties, equipment lease pricing, state of the art equipment purchase contracts for Corporate Banking, Corporate Finance, International, and Corporate Services.

Overall responsibility for the legal functions relating to corporate practice, governance, and insurance. Particular emphasis on anti-takeover, 16b, and Corporate Code of Conduct issues. Designed and executed revisions of the director/officer liability and indemnification policy.

Served as a task-force chair for a compliance review of all company owned real estate with sale and lease-back requirements including title insurance and surveys.

Developed three non-qualified management incentive plans with related deferred funds and three non-qualified performance unit plans. Sole in-house counsel on numerous pension, stock option, 401(K), ESOP, Supplemental Executive, and welfare benefit plans.

Continued

ROBIN HUGHES   Page 2

EDUCATION:

UNIVERSITY OF CALIFORNIA, SAN DIEGO
J.D. 1980
Editor of Law Review submissions committee

UNIVERSITY OF FLORIDA
B.A. SOCIOLOGY 1977

Admitted to the California and Nevada Bars.

References available upon request

ROSEMARY SYSQUENTHIS
45 BRIGHTON WAY
KINGSTON, KS 88446
(709)555-8833

EDUCATION   UNIVERSITY OF KANSAS
MARKLAND SCHOOL OF LAW
J.D. 1985
Honors: 1985 Writing Competition
        1984 Writing Competition

KANSAS STATE UNIVERSITY
B.A., Mathematics & Philosophy, 1982

EXPERIENCE   KANTER, BROWN & TODD
SENIOR ASSOCIATE 1986-Present

Serve as a senior associate for a mid-sized defense firm specializing in medical malpractice litigation. Conduct legal and medical research and draft memoranda. Analyze prior testimony of medical experts called to testify against our clients. Reduce large depositions to digest form and prepare litigation binders. Attend trials and provide assistance to lead counsel.

HONORABLE JOHN GAYS
SUPREME COURT OF KANSAS
LAW CLERK 1985-1986

Prepared memoranda on issues in pending cases. Researched the insurability of Rule 111 sanctions, the admissibility of victim impact statements, and the validity of family exclusion clauses in automobile insurance contracts.

HONORABLE GUY HANDLER
UNITED STATES DISTRICT JUDGE
LAW INTERN Summer 1984

Researched law and helped draft memoranda, orders, and opinions. Areas researched included collateral estoppel, habeas corpus, and the use of the Paperwork Reduction Act of 1980 as a defense to federal income tax evasion. Attended pretrial conferences, jury selections, hearings, and trials.

CRAIN WATERS RESORT
HEAD WAITER Summers 1982, 1983

Served customers, trained new employees, and catered all banquets and receptions.

DALTON SAMPLES
22 LONG ROAD
DETROIT, MI 45775   (607)555-8833

ALLIED CHEMICAL AND PETROLEUM COMPANY

GENERAL COUNSEL   1981-Present

Reduced substantial backlog of litigation and successfully managed affairs of the company to avoid significant new lawsuits despite challenging and changing business environments.

Employed innovative approaches to obtain directors' and officers' liability insurance during turbulent times for the company.

Restructured controllership function thereby increasing productivity in the consolidation area by 30%.

Authorized development, evaluated, and approved implementation of inventory cycle counting procedures, eliminating need for annual physical inventory.

Decreased outside audit fees 23% by more effectively coordinating internal and external audits, implementing a plant self audit program, and revising audit scope coverage.

Created the company's Internal Specialist Program. High potential individuals were given responsibility over specific legal areas. Specialists gained international experience and established key legal policies. Current staff was able to meet expanded needs.

LODSTRUM INDUSTRIES
Director of Taxes   1977-1981

Responsible for minimizing worldwide tax liability and exploiting tax planning opportunities. Key responsibilities included excess foreign tax credit utilization; expatriate tax planning; inter-company pricing; international treaty provisions; legal entity capitalization alternatives; short and long-term incentive arrangements; technology agreements; as well as federal, state, local, and foreign tax compliance.

Handled domestic and international tax research and planning covering audit negotiations, depreciation, and foreign tax credits. This included inventory absorption, redemption, reorganizations, and ruling requests.

Assumed a leadership role in the National Association of Lawyers and the Federation of Schools of Legal training.

Continued

DALTON SAMPLES   **Page 2**

EDUCATION

J.D. UNIVERSITY OF DETROIT

M.S. FINANCE, UNIVERSITY OF MICHIGAN

M.B.A. (Concentration in Finance), DETROIT COLLEGE

B.A., ECONOMICS, DETROIT COLLEGE

ADDITIONAL TRAINING

STANFORD UNIVERSITY: FINANCIAL MANAGEMENT PROGRAM

KELLOGG BUSINESS SCHOOL: MANAGERIAL NEGOTIATIONS

LARR ASSOCIATES: INTENSIVE EXECUTIVE DEVELOPMENT SEMINAR

Chapter Six

SAMPLE COVER LETTERS

November 30, 19__

Carl Boardman
23 Trautman Rd.
Summerville, TX   64332

Jason Colt
Harden & Stone
55 Stone St
Houston, TX   33445

Dear Mr. Colt,

As a recent graduate of the University of Texas Law School, I am seeking an associate position with Harden & Stone.

I have worked as a Texas Adult Probation and Parole Officer for a little over four years. This experience has given me valuable insights and experiences into the criminal justice system. I have gained a practical knowledge of the functions of the judicial system and have personally experienced courtroom methods and tactics. Further, as a probation officer, I have had the opportunity to interact with a wide variety of individuals and gain helpful insights into their methods, motivations, and thought processes.

Enclosed is my resume for your review. I would like to be a litigator with your firm and feel that I could bring a great deal of knowledge, skill, and enthusiasm.

Thank you for your time and consideration. I look forward to talking with you further.

Sincerely,

Carl Boardman

January 30, 19__

Carl Bohley
556 Young Ave.
Washington, DC   22338

Edward St. Marks
Thomas Littlefield Associates
Begin, TX   44566

Dear Mr. St. Marks,

Since last September, I have been working as a minority counsel on the United States Senate Committee on Commerce as a Jack Griswald legal fellow. The fellowship concludes this September and I am writing to inquire about a position with your firm. I am a member of the Texas Bar and am seeking a position to practice commercial litigation, trademark, or antitrust law.

On the Commerce Committee, I handled matters for the Aviation, Surface Transportation, and Consumer Subcommittees. I have also had experience as a summer law clerk in a large law firm and as a research assistant for a law professor. Moreover, I was highly successful in law school and finished in the top ten percent of my class. I was inducted into the Order of the Coif and served as managing Editor of the Journal of Urban and Contemporary Law.

I appreciate your consideration of my candidacy. I look forward to hearing from you.

Sincerely,

Carl Bohley

March 14, 19___

Wendall Douras
55 Tall Rd.
Miami, FL 44556

George Table
Range, Justin & Jung
Vicey, Florida 55432

Dear Mr. Table,

Enclosed please find my resume.

I am interested in a either a part-time or full-time position with your law firm.

I am a licensed attorney and recently passed the Florida Bar Exam.

Additionally, I am a Certified Public Accountant and will be receiving my L.L.M. degree in Taxation in May.

Please contact me if any additional information is needed.

Sincerely,

Wendell Douras

June 4, 19__

August Ford
34 Ring Rd.
St. Louis, MO   64553

Jason Rugo
Gallup, Harold & Huey
St. Louis, MO   63102

Dear Mr. Rugo,

I am an Army judge advocate voluntarily leaving active duty this year to pursue employment with a firm in the St. Louis area. My application to waive into the Missouri Bar is being processed by the Clerk of the Missouri Supreme Court.

My resume is attached for your consideration as an associate. I have a varied legal background with significant exposure to a broad range of litigation including civil and criminal experience in state and federal courts and administrative tribunals. I have personally litigated more than twenty cases. In my current position as Staff Attorney with the National Security Agency, I served as lead agency counsel in the successful prosecution of General Trio and the wrongful death litigation arising out of the bombing of the Trans American Airlines flight #34.

I will be in St. Louis the week of May 23rd and would welcome the opportunity to interview or meet informally with you or a member of your firm. Please expect my telephone call within the next week to discuss employment possibilities. Thank you for your courtesies.

Sincerely,

August Ford

August 6, 19__

Renu Gupta
34 Tonkin Lane
Sandy Spring, MO   64332

Donald Fallup
Fallup & Young
101 S. Early St.
St Louis, MO   65443

Dear Mr. Fallup,

I am a graduate of the University of Missouri school of law and am a licensed Missouri attorney searching for employment in the St. Louis area. Enclosed is a copy of my resume and law school transcript for your review.

As the enclosed resume details, I have been employed by the Kansas City law firm of Lacy & Yeaster since August of 1990. Prior to that position I was a law clerk for the Honorable Kevin Marshall of the Missouri Court of Appeals for the Western District of Missouri. I graduated from law school in the top 20% of my class and served as a Note and Comment Editor on the Missouri Law Review.

I will be available for an interview at your convenience to discuss my qualifications and experience. I look forward to hearing from you soon.

Sincerely,

Renu Gupta

September 4, 19__

Jim Brinkman
23 Park Ave.
New York, NY 80054

Alan Jones
Johnston & Ferry
34 Terry Rd.
Lincoln, MA 01773

Dear Mr. Jones,

During a meeting with Jack Carson last week, he discussed your firm's history and recent growth. He suggested I write to you. While he was not sure that you had an immediate need for someone like me, he did feel that we might have a mutual interest in getting together for a brief meeting.

To give you a better picture of what I can contribute, I've enclosed a copy of my resume, which discusses my experience and potential contributions.

I would welcome a brief meeting with you to discuss what specific contributions I could make to your organization. I'll call you on Monday to see when such a meeting might be set up.

Sincerely,

Jim Brinkman

October 2, 19__

Margaret Carson
6 River Run Dr.
Destin, FL 77889

Karen Barnes
KBS Legal Services
123 Altoona Drive
Gulf Shores, AL 44567

Dear Ms. Barnes,

A mutual friend, Sharon Greisse, suggested I contact you
concerning potential legal openings within your firm.

After raising a family of 4, I returned to law school and
received my J.D. in 1984. Since then I have been an associate
with Trasco & Taylor in Huntsville. Unfortunately this is a
branch office of the firm and economic conditions dictate
that the firm will be consolidating its operations in Dallas
in June. Since I desire to remain in Alabama, I declined the
firm's offer to relocate to Texas.

I would welcome the opportunity to meet with you in the near
future to discuss any opportunities which may exist within
your organization or other leads that you may know of.

I'll call your office next week to follow up.

Sincerely,

Margaret Carson

November 5, 19__

Jerry Fano
55 Tully Ave.
Houston, TX 23998

Mark Carl
Jennings Corporation
123 Willow Springs
Houston, TX 23998

Dear Mr. Carl,

Jennings Corporation has an excellent reputation in the manufacturing industry and is known for their quality products. Due to a recent downsizing at Gorman Products, I am currently seeking a position in the corporate legal staff in an organization like yours. I believe I can make a valuable contribution to your company by using my 25 years of experience to help further your rapid growth and good service.

As an experienced attorney, I have worked with many different types of issues that impact manufacturing companies such as yours.

I will call you early next week to set up an appointment to discuss employment opportunities. I look forward to talking with you then.

Sincerely,

Jerry Fano

March 3, 19__

John Fitzgerald
5 Lafter St.
Detroit, MI   33445

David Schuster
Gotham Industries
445 Milk St.
Detroit, MI 55677

Dear Mr. Schuster,

I am writing you concerning your opening in the legal department. As my resume outlines I have had extensive experience in this function. Some of my accomplishments include the following:

> Directed development of a Fortune 500 company's five year legal strategic plan.

> Developed and presented legal proposals to the corporate executive committee.

> Conducted a market research study on the impact of legal solutions on the local business community.

> Created and managed the legal department for a major manufacturer.

> Designed operational flow charts, tracking systems, and productivity measurements.

> Lectured on legal principles to groups of 30 to 90 people.

I have worked cery successfully in diverse and challenging environments. I look forward to meeting you in person to discuss how my talents can lead to superior results for you. I will call you next week to arrange a convenient time.

Sincerely,

John Fitzgerald

April 8, 19__

Becky Flynn
33 Rush St.
Wichita, KS   77533

Jason Roberts
Luskin Department Stores
45 Lucky St.
Wichita, KS 77658

Dear Mr. Roberts,

After more than 30 years of experience in the legal field, I am seeking a new position where my abilities can be utilized more fully.

As you can see from the attached resume, my record is one of increasing responsibility. My most recent employer has commented favorably on my in-depth knowledge of how the law impacts their business plans and the assistance they have received from my efforts.

If you see a possible fit with your organization, I would like to meet with you for an exploratory discussion.

I'll plan to call you next week to see when we might get together.

Sincerely,

Becky Flynn

July 6, 19__

Andy Freidenberg
22 Winter St.
Omaha, NE 55676

Commissioner Arnold Stranley
Lincoln County
234 Main St.
Omaha, NE 55699

Dear Commissioner Stranley,

I have been a resident of Lincoln County for more than 20 years. Most of those years I have been employed within the county. I am writing to ask for your help. As a knowledgeable leader in the county's efforts to bring additional industry to Lincoln, you may be aware of organizations in need of proven talent in the legal profession.

The enclosed resume illustrates my progression of increasingly responsible assignments since graduating from law school in 1961. I am most interested in finding a position as a Vice President of Legal Affairs for a medium size manufacturing operation.

I would like to meet with you to discuss companies or people you think I should talk with in my search. I will follow up next week to request an appointment.

Sincerely,

Andy Freidenberg

September 14, 19__

Yolanda Peterson
34 Ross Rd.
St. Louis, MO 64332

Paul Kamikahara
Cordell Bank
St. Louis, MO 65445

Dear Mr. Kamikahara,

I recently read in the Washington University Alumni letter that you were in need of a senior attorney. For over the past twenty years I have worked as a partner for one of New York's premier law firms. For personal lifestyle reasons my family and I have decided to relocate to the St. Louis area.

I've enclosed a copy of my resume which further outlines my background and experience. I'll give you a call the week of May 5th, to determine the appropriate next steps.

Best Wishes,

Yolanda Peterson

May 5, 19__

Pat Lee
20 Young St.
Los Angeles, CA 98665

David Alan
Jones Consulting
556 Glengo Dr.
Los Angeles, CA 987667

Dear Mr. Alan,

Jack Jones suggested I contact you concerning assistance with a career change. I am a highly experienced attorney looking for a position with a firm that understands what it takes to succeed in today's marketplace.

As the enclosed resume illustrates, with more than 30 years experience in a variety of working situations, I offer a solid background in both law firm and corporate environments.

I would greatly appreciate any information or referrals you could provide. I am convinced that networking will be the key to successfully finding the right position. Can we get together for 15-20 minutes sometime next week? I will call you in the next several days to schedule an appointment at your convenience.

Sincerely,

Pat Lee

December 5, 19__

John Parson
77 Title St.
Dothan, AL 66455

Paula Yetle
Thomas, Hole & Wall
Gibens, AL 66785

Dear Ms. Yetle,

I am interested in being considered for any appropriate positions which may be available with your firm.

My practical administrative law experience comes from a legal internship in the Washington, D.C. office of Congressman Joe Daley. I was responsible for various legislative issues including criminal victim restitution, military procurement, and the federal antitrust laws. My international law experience is from a research position with the Conservative Party in London, England, and through an intensive semester of study with the University of Gouldon London Law Program.

I will follow up with you the week of the 21st and look forward to speaking with you at that time.

Sincerely,

John Parson

September 5, 19__

Neal Donald
Barny & Maze
Tomas, IL   60045

Dear Mr. Donald,

I am a 1988 graduate of Norwich University School of Law and am a member of the Illinois Bar. I have a strong background in the general practice of law along with unique experience in administrative and international law. I wish to utilize my experience in a position with your firm as a litigator or negotiator in the field of labor, business, administrative, or international law.

My practical experience includes a year as the law clerk of Mr. Thomas Gould, a litigator for the firm Hos, Hemm and Hoe. While working with Mr. Gould I dealt with cases involving bankruptcy, contracts, constitutional law, insurance law, libel, personal injury, products liability, and wills. As a law student I worked on all allowable aspects of Mr. Gould's cases, writing briefs and other legal documents, interviewing clients, and researching the law.

I have strong litigation and interpersonal skills and hope to use my experience to benefit your firm. I am also willing to discuss the possibility of doing work for your firm as an independent contractor or in some other type of alternative employment arrangement if this is more desirable. I will contact you during the week of April 19th to discuss employment opportunities with your firm. I look forward to speaking with you.

Sincerely,

Harold Prewitt

October 16, 19__

Nancy Escobar
33 Thomas St.
Luskin, CT   08997

Tom Rander
Garner & Young
Billings, CT   09665

Dear Mr. Rander,

I am an attorney currently entering my fourth year of law practice. I plan to relocate to the Billings area where my fiance's family resides, and I am very interested in obtaining employment as an associate with your firm.

As my enclosed resume reflects, I am presently employed as an associate with the firm of Allen & Allen. In this position I have prepared many cases from beginning to end. My responsibilities have included motion and trial practice and I have extensive experience in the areas of pleading, discovery, and legal research.

I am a graduate of the University of Lincoln College of Law, where I was a member of the Law Review and ranked in the top one-third of my class. I also have a degree in business administration which I have found useful in corporate and business related legal matters.

I am extremely motivated and believe I can make a valuable contribution to your office. I am available for an interview at your convenience. I look forward to hearing from you soon.

Sincerely,

Nancy Escobar

December 12, 19__

Leslie Rush
66 Iron St.
Beacon, MD   05443

Malvina Atwood
Nathan Harold Associates
Thomasville, MD   03445

Dera Ms. Atwood,

I am presently an associate at Milken & Miles where I focus on appellate law. I realize that you receive many resumes from qualified attorneys; however, I believe I have exceptional qualifications for a position requiring extensive legal analysis and writing. Thus, I enclose my resume for your review. Briefly, it reflects my strong academic background, graduating Phi Beta Kappa, and extensive legal experience.

I would certainly appreciate the opportunity to meet with you at your convenience to discuss my qualifications for a position at your firm. Thank you for your consideration.

Sincerely,

Leslie Rush

June 4, 19__

Becky Sipple
22 Wright St.
Houston, TX 43554

Michael Kahn
Kahn, Cuin & Tobb
Houston, TX 44556

Dear Mr. Kahn,

I am writing to express my interest in employment with your firm as an associate. Your firm's excellent reputation and my interest in civil litigation prompted this letter.

As the enclosed resume indicates, I am currently clerking for Chief Judge George Young of the United States District Court. I am a licensed in Texas and will be available to begin work upon completion of my clerkship in August.

I would welcome the opportunity to meet with you at your convenience and discuss any openings the firm might have. I look forward to hearing from you soon.

Sincerely,

Becky Sipple

June 21, 19__

Bruce Weber
77 Red Range Rd.
Tulsa, OK   54332

Barbara Gold
Gold, Remaid & Wilson
Tulsa, OK   55677

Dear Ms. Gold,

I am a law student at Tulsa University with an expected graduation
of spring of next year. I am writing to inquire about a possible
summer position with your firm. My wife and I wish to settle in the
Tulsa area and have extensive family and social ties in the region.

I possess good writing skills which I will further enhance next fall
by participating in a Judicial Clerkship clinical course. Additionally,
I intend to utilize my accounting degree in law practice and am
scheduled to take the CPA examination this spring prior to
graduation.

Enclosed is a resume detailed by experience and background. I would
appreciate the opportunity to meet with you and further discuss my
credentials. If you require additional information regarding my
qualifications, I invite you to contact any of the references listed.
Thank you for your consideration. I look forward to hearing from you.

Sincerely,

Bruce Weber

VGM CAREER BOOKS

CAREER DIRECTORIES
Careers Encyclopedia
Dictionary of Occupational
Titles
Occupational Outlook
Handbook

CAREERS FOR
Animal Lovers
Bookworms
Computer Buffs
Crafty People
Culture Lovers
Environmental Types
Film Buffs
Foreign Language Aficionados
Good Samaritans
Gourmets
History Buffs
Kids at Heart
Nature Lovers
Night Owls
Number Crunchers
Plant Lovers
Shutterbugs
Sports Nuts
Travel Buffs

CAREERS IN
Accounting; Advertising;
Business; Child Care;
Communications; Computers;
Education; Engineering;
the Environment; Finance;
Government; Health Care;
High Tech; Journalism; Law;
Marketing; Medicine;
Science; Social &
Rehabilitation Services

CAREER PLANNING
Admissions Guide to Selective
Business Schools
Beating Job Burnout
Beginning Entrepreneur
Career Planning &
Development for College
Students & Recent Graduates
Career Change

Careers Checklists
Cover Letters They Don't
Forget
Executive Job Search Strategies
Guide to Basic Cover Letter
Writing
Guide to Basic Resume Writing
Guide to Temporary
Employment
Job Interviews Made Easy
Joyce Lain Kennedy's Career
Book
Out of Uniform
Resumes Made Easy
Slam Dunk Resumes
Successful Interviewing for
College Seniors
Time for a Change

CAREER PORTRAITS
Animals   Nursing
Cars   Sports
Computers   Teaching
Music   Travel

GREAT JOBS FOR
Communications Majors
English Majors
Foreign Language Majors
History Majors
Psychology Majors

HOW TO
Approach an Advertising
Agency and Walk Away with
the Job You Want
Bounce Back Quickly After
Losing Your Job
Choose the Right Career
Find Your New Career Upon
Retirement
Get & Keep Your First Job
Get Hired Today
Get into the Right Business
School
Get into the Right Law School
Get People to Do Things Your
Way
Have a Winning Job Interview

Hit the Ground Running in
Your New Job
Improve Your Study Skills
Jump Start a Stalled Career
Land a Better Job
Launch Your Career in TV
News
Make the Right Career Moves
Market Your College Degree
Move from College into a
Secure Job
Negotiate the Raise You
Deserve
Prepare a Curriculum Vitae
Prepare for College
Run Your Own Home Business
Succeed in College
Succeed in High School
Write a Winning Resume
Write Successful Cover Letters
Write Term Papers & Reports
Write Your College Application
Essay

OPPORTUNITIES IN
This extensive series provides
detailed information on nearly
150 individual career fields.

RESUMES FOR
Advertising Careers
Banking and Financial Careers
Business Management Careers
College Students &
Recent Graduates
Communications Careers
Education Careers
Engineering Careers
Environmental Careers
50 + Job Hunters
Health and Medical Careers
High School Graduates
High Tech Careers
Law Careers
Midcareer Job Changes
Sales and Marketing Careers
Scientific and Technical Careers
Social Service Careers
The First-Time Job Hunter

 **VGM Career Horizons**
a division of *NTC Publishing Group*
4255 West Touhy Avenue
Lincolnwood, Illinois 60646–1975